modern comfort food

modern comfort food

a Barefoot Contessa cookbook

ina garten

photographs by Quentin Bacon

party photographs by Jean-Pierre Uys

clarkson potter/publishers

new york

Published in the United States by
Clarkson Potter/Publishers, an imprint
of Random House, a division of Penguin
Random House LLC, New York.
clarksonpotter.com

CLARKSON POTTER is a trademark
and POTTER with colophon is a
registered trademark of
Penguin Random House LLC.

Library of Congress Cataloging-in-
Publication Data is available upon
request.

ISBN 978-0-8041-8706-0
Ebook ISBN 978-0-8041-8707-7
Premium edition ISBN 978-593-23279-3

Printed in China

Book design by Marysarah Quinn
Photographs by Quentin Bacon
Photographs on pages 2–3, 4, 22, 24, 26,
27, 28–29, 100–01, 102–03, and 248–49,
by Jean-Pierre Uys

10 9 8 7 6 5 4 3 2 1

FIRST EDITION

contents

thank you!

Could this possibly be my twelfth cookbook?? I started writing *The Barefoot Contessa Cookbook* in 1997 and the team that worked on the photographs for that first book—Melanie Acevedo, Rori Trovato, and Denise Canter—taught me so much about photographing food. I'll always be grateful to them for those exciting days we had together.

Twenty years later, I still work with amazing people. My own team for this book is Lidey Heuck, Kristina Felix Ibarra, and—although she *thought* she was retiring—I convinced my longtime assistant Barbara Libath to continue retesting recipes to make sure they're *really* perfect. Sarah Leah Chase writes her own wonderful cookbooks and also works with me on mine. I love my team and feel so lucky to work with them.

Thanks to my longtime publisher Clarkson Potter; no one creates more beautiful cookbooks. We've been together since my first book and I'm so grateful for the love and support of David Drake, Aaron Wehner, Susan Corcoran, Doris Cooper, Kate Tyler, and Raquel Pelzel. But most of all, my longtime editor Pam Krauss and book designer Marysarah Quinn get the credit for putting up with my obsessions all these years. I'd be lost without them.

The team of people who photograph my cookbooks just gets better and better. Quentin Bacon is the amazing photographer. Christine Albano with her assistant Dylan Going cooked all the gorgeous food and my long-time friend Miguel Flores-Vianna styled all the photographs. Jean-Pierre Uys shot the beautiful photographs of my party that are sprinkled through the book. Thank you for all your hard work and dedication.

And finally thank you to my incredible agent, Esther Newberg, who takes such good care of me; and my adorable husband, Jeffrey, who is my constant advisor and taste-tester!

BAREFOOT CONTESSA FAMILY STYLE

barefoot contessa foolproof

the barefoot contessa cookbook

barefoot contessa *how easy is that?*

ina garten | make it ahead

ina garten | cooking for Jeffrey

barefoot contessa at home

BAREFOOT IN PARIS

barefoot contessa back to basics

BAREFOOT CONTESSA PARTIES!

THE
*NEW YORK
TIMES*
BESTSELLING
AUTHOR

ina garten
cook like a pro
recipes & tips for home cooks
a barefoot contessa cookbook

SMASHED EGGS ON TOAST

what is it about comfort food?

I often say that you can be miserable before eating a cookie and you can be miserable after eating a cookie, but you can never be miserable *while* you're eating a cookie. And while I say that half-jokingly, the sentiment is true. Food has an almost magical ability to comfort us, soothe us, and bring us together in so many ways. We celebrate special occasions with food—a birthday cake or a big roast turkey—and we also turn to food for comfort on not-so-happy occasions, a delivery of baked goods to a family member who's under the weather, or a homemade dinner for a friend having a rough time. Food can be so much more than simple sustenance.

So, what exactly is comfort food? It's food that's not just nourishing but it's also emotionally satisfying. After September 11, 2001, I can't tell you how many people told me they went out to get all the ingredients to make my Outrageous Brownies from *The Barefoot Contessa Cookbook*. After the financial crisis in 2008, restaurants everywhere suffered as customers cut back on their spending. But fast-food places prospered because they served inexpensive classics like hamburgers and French fries. As I write this, we're in the middle of a global pandemic and I have no idea when it will end or what devastation it will cause. People are isolated and stressed. Everyone I know has stocked up their fridges and pantries with ingredients they can cook for weeks or even months—chickens, vegetables, fruits, beans, rice, and dried legumes. But my friend Deborah Davis commented that she opens her fridge and looks at all the healthy food in there, and all she wants is a grilled cheese sandwich! I can totally relate to that! During times of financial and political stress, there's something about a hamburger and Coke or a big bowl of beef stew that just makes us feel better. They're not fancy—in fact, quite the opposite. They're familiar, delicious, and soul-satisfying. In other words, they're comfort food.

There are many foods that are universally comforting. I think we can probably all agree that a mixed green salad isn't anyone's idea of comfort food. But chicken soup? Every international cuisine has its own version: Greek avgolemono soup, Vietnamese chicken pho, Belgian waterzooi, and my personal favorite, chicken soup with matzo balls. For this book, I developed Chicken Pot Pie Soup (page 58), a mash-up of classic chicken soup and chicken pot pie that hits all the right notes when you're tired or cranky.

Comfort foods are often the dishes that transcend cultures and borders. Many popular foods that have become ingrained in American culture—ramen, tacos, pizza—were originally brought to this country by immigrants who sought to re-create the comforting taste of home. Many of the recipes in this book are inspired by comfort foods from around the world—from Emily's English Roasted Potatoes (page 171) to Shrimp & Linguine Fra Diavolo (page 130) to Cheesy Chicken Enchiladas (page 114).

CHEESY CHICKEN ENCHILADAS

Comfort food may be different for each person. An egg salad sandwich on toasted rye can cheer me up on a bad day, but it might not be what does it for you! Often the foods we turn to for comfort are rooted in what we ate as children. Peanut butter and jelly sandwiches are the classic American lunch for kids but when I offered to make them for my British film crew, they recoiled in horror. Instead, they offered to make me *their* classic childhood lunch—white bread with cold baked beans from a can and Kraft singles on top. Yikes! (Please don't tell them but I'll take a PB&J any day!)

Lots of the recipes in this book evoke old-fashioned American foods that many of us remember from our childhoods. My mother used to make canned split pea soup with cut-up hot dogs in it (I know it sounds bizarre, but I thought it was delicious). I've updated it by making homemade Split Pea Soup with Crispy Kielbasa (page 62). The soup is filled with lots of vegetables and flavored with a smoked ham hock and sautéed kielbasa. It's basically the grown-up version of the soup my mother made, but so much more satisfying.

I polled my friends and you'd be surprised how many said their go-to comfort food was a tuna fish sandwich and potato chips (in one case, the potato chips went *in* the sandwich!). So I knew I had to include a recipe for a tuna melt in this book that was nostal-

ULTIMATE TUNA MELTS

gic but better than the diner classic. My Ultimate Tuna Melts (page 79) are made with really good imported tuna and have melted cheese and microgreens on top. Jeffrey's favorite comfort food—tomato soup and a grilled cheese sandwich—was the inspiration for both my Creamy Tomato Bisque (page 83) with a hint of saffron and the Cheddar & Chutney Grilled Cheese (page 84). You don't need to have a bad day to love these two together.

So, that's what makes dishes comfort food, but I had to ask myself, what makes the recipes in this book modern?? When I'm working on a

APPLESAUCE CAKE WITH BOURBON RAISINS

recipe, I like to start with a remembered flavor and spend time researching how the dish was traditionally made. Then, I figure out how I can update that dish—whether it's lightening up the recipe, making it easier to cook, or simply adding more modern flavors, such as Sriracha and pomegranate. I wanted each dish in this book to feel familiar but be so much more delicious than you expected. And I realized that while comfort food is the focus of this particular book, that's what I'm always looking for in a recipe: true home cooking but with a twist or update that makes it special enough to serve to company.

For example, I wanted to make a classic beef stew, but in my experience beef stew can be pretty boring—with tough or stringy chunks of beef and a thin, bland tomato sauce. I knew it could be so much better! In order to update that American classic, I borrowed ingredients from two other dishes I love—beef Bourguignon and braised short ribs. Instead of starting by searing bacon, I used pancetta, which has a great flavor without the smokiness of bacon. Then, I swapped the usual beef chuck for boneless short ribs, which added a richness that made everything, particularly the sauce, so much more delicious. And finally, I added a bottle of good red wine and a splash of Cognac to give the sauce more depth of flavor. Now whenever I serve my Ultimate Beef Stew (page 104), my guests say they'll never make beef stew any other way again.

One of my personal favorite comfort foods is a BLT. It's classic diner food, and just fine as is, but when I'm entertaining I like to make a new version that's really over the top. For my Lobster BLTs (page 80), I use applewood-smoked bacon, ripe summer tomatoes, creamy Hass avocados, good bakery white bread, Thousand Island dressing, and, of course, perfectly poached lobster. They're good and messy to eat but everyone loves the old-fashioned flavor of BLTs with this more elegant, grown-up spin. It's comfort food dressed up for company.

When you're having a dinner party, it can be tempting to make something fancy to impress your guests. But when I tell my friends that I'm making Truffled Mac & Cheese (page 138) or Smashed Hamburgers with Caramelized Onions (page 116) for dinner, and Applesauce Cake with Bourbon Raisins (page 198) for dessert, they light up with glee. I might order cassoulet or grilled octopus at a restaurant, but at home we all want something simple and satisfying. The look on my friends' faces when they see me bring Baked Rigatoni with Lamb Ragù (page 134) to the table says it all.

One of the dinners I love on a cold winter night is sausage and peppers with polenta. What I don't love is frying sausages on the stove and turning my kitchen into one big oil slick! Instead, for my Roasted Sausages, Peppers & Onions (page 121), I found a way to make the whole thing in the oven. You set a timer and forget about it—and no mess to clean up! Spicy cooked sausages, lots of onions and peppers, and if you serve it with a big puddle of my creamy Fresh Corn Polenta (page 172), your guests will be very happy.

BRUSSELS SPROUTS PIZZA CARBONARA

Another way I make comfort food more modern is by finding new ways to serve dishes we all know and love. Everybody associates Hollandaise sauce with eggs Benedict, but for my Roasted Shishito Peppers with Easy Hollandaise (page 168), I serve the classic French sauce with a vegetable that's kind of new to me—shishito peppers. I love the rich, lemony sauce with the mild heat of the peppers. And instead of standing over a double boiler to make Hollandaise on the stove or dragging out my blender, I developed a way to make it with just a bowl and a small whisk—in the microwave! So easy!

Sometimes, simply adding a fresh ingredient to a classic dish will make it seem more modern. For my Brussels Sprouts Pizza Carbonara (page 129), I started with pizza dough from the local pizzeria (instead of making it from scratch!), spread on a rich carbonara sauce with lots of Italian Pecorino cheese, and topped it all with thinly shaved Brussels sprouts.

The creamy sauce and piquant cheese are the perfect combination with the sprouts, which get crispy and sweet when you bake the pizza. We all love a big bowl of spaghetti carbonara but it is so rich that I need a nap afterward. I added fresh spring vegetables like asparagus, snap peas, and fresh English peas to the carbonara and came up with a modern twist on a classic—Spring Green Spaghetti Carbonara (page 137).

I don't know about you, but I have to admit that these days, I'm a little grumpier than I used to be. I've always loved reading the newspaper in the morning but now it feels as though it's only bad news. Friends are angry with each other. People are venting on Twitter. It's all just so stressful. So, what do we do about it?? We reach for a cold martini, or a pint of rum raisin Häagen-Dazs ice cream to soothe our hurt feelings. This book is devoted to helping you serve up seriously satisfying and delicious food that will feed not only your cravings but also your soul. I hope it will help you take care of yourself *and* the people around you so everyone is happier and less stressed. In this crazy world, that's an incredible gift you can give to yourself, your family, and your friends. Cooking really delicious comfort food—particularly fresh, modern comfort food—ensures that everyone at your table will feel happy and satisfied, and isn't that how we want the people we love to feel? I know I do!!

SPRING GREEN SPAGHETTI CARBONARA

xxxx Ina

good ingredients

People tease me because I call for "good ingredients." I know, why would you use bad ingredients?? I started calling for specific ingredients because they do make a difference when you're cooking. They don't have to be expensive but they need to be chosen thoughtfully; which olive oil tastes the freshest and which vanilla delivers the best flavor to balance the sweet chocolate?

Salt is probably the most important ingredient of all and some taste saltier than others. In fact, even different kosher salts have different degrees of saltiness. I use Diamond Crystal kosher salt for all my cooking and baking. David's and Morton kosher salts are actually saltier and if you use them, you'll need to cut back on the measurements. I also recommend French sea salt called fleur de sel and British Maldon flaked sea salt for finishing because of their unique flavor and texture. Which salt you choose will determine how much of it you'll need to use for the dish to be perfectly seasoned.

HELLMANN'S OR BEST
FOODS MAYONNAISE

DIAMOND CRYSTAL
KOSHER SALT

MALDON
SEA SALT

EXTRA-LARGE
ORGANIC EGGS

GREY POUPON OR MAILLE
DIJON MUSTARD

FRESH HERBS

TELLICHERRY BLACK
PEPPERCORNS

SAN MARZANO CANNED
TOMATOES

NIELSEN-MASSEY PURE
VANILLA EXTRACT

OLIO SANTO OLIVE OIL

DE CECCO PASTA

GOYA CHIPOTLE PEPPERS
IN ADOBO SAUCE

BAR HARBOR
SEAFOOD STOCK

ITALIAN PARMESAN
CHEESE

FRESHLY SQUEEZED
LEMON JUICE

HOMEMADE CHICKEN
STOCK (PAGE 64)

cocktails

hot spiced apple cider

—

ultimate bloody marys

—

frozen palomas

—

pomegranate gimlets

—

potato galettes with smoked salmon

—

fig & cheese toasts

—

warm spinach & artichoke dip

—

fresh crab nachos

—

cacio e pepe cheese puffs

—

grilled oysters with lemon dill butter

—

spicy pimento cheese spread

—

kielbasa with mustard dip

—

modern entertaining

A few years ago, Jeffrey and I were invited to a very elegant dinner party. I knew there would be really interesting people and the conversation would be amazing, which it was. When we arrived, we were greeted by butlers serving cocktails and hors d'oeuvres from silver trays; it was all incredibly beautiful and impressive. But when we sat down, my heart sank; the enormous table was set with silver chargers topped with English china dinner plates, and lots of polished silver flatware—plus *six* elegant crystal glasses. I knew immediately there would be six courses coming with six different wines and we were going to be sitting at that table for a very long time! That kind of formality tends to make me more worried about knocking over a glass of red wine than connecting with other guests. Isn't that why we have dinner parties in the first place?

For me, entertaining is a much more pared down and free-flowing affair. It's about making people feel relaxed and at ease, no matter what the occasion. Recently, I hosted a big cocktail party fund-raiser in East Hampton. I decided to do it in a more modern way that kept things fun and casual. I set up the long kitchen counter in the barn with platters piled high with fruit, cheese, crackers, roasted shrimp with cocktail sauce, big baskets of store-bought cheese straws, and sliced smoked salmon with breads. Almost everything was assembled or at most, simply cooked. The one thing we made was Cacio e Pepe Cheese Puffs (page 47) so the barn smelled wonderful when people arrived; and there was one hot appetizer. In the library, I set up a bar table with a huge silver tub of ice packed with bottles of California rosé and sparkling water. I set out all-purpose stemmed wine glasses and let everyone help themselves. The music was cranked up; people wandered around the garden, talked with friends, enjoyed a glass of wine, and had a wonderful time. And because I'd kept things simple—and didn't have to worry about plating the hors d'oeuvres or refilling everyone's glasses—I had fun, too!

Whether it's a cocktail party for a hundred or a few good friends coming for dinner, my goal is to make my guests feel relaxed and happy. When I invite friends for a small dinner party, I set up a bar in the living

room so everyone can mix their own drinks. We hang out with casual hors d'oeuvres like guacamole or Fig & Cheese Toasts (page 40) that we all pass around. I have a formal dining room but we usually eat dinner in the kitchen so I can cook, serve, and still be at my own party. I like to set my 48-inch round table for six so we're all cozy together and it's easy to talk. Flowers and candles are low so you can see each other across the table. Nights like that are soul-satisfying for me. No matter what else is going on in my life—or in the world—if I get that right, I know I'll feel better. For me, that's what modern entertaining is all about: taking the time to enjoy good food and good conversation with the people I love. I hope this book helps you do the same thing for the people that matter the most to you.

hot spiced apple cider

Is there anything more comforting on a cold, snowy day than sitting in front of a roaring fire with a good book and a delicious hot drink to warm your insides? With all its wintery spices like cinnamon, cloves, and star anise, you could certainly make this hot spiced apple cider alcohol-free, but good bourbon is so perfect in it, why would you??

MAKES 5 OR 6 DRINKS

4 cups fresh apple cider

4 whole black peppercorns

6 or 7 (2 to 3-inch) cinnamon sticks

3 whole dried cloves

1 star anise

1 navel orange

Good bourbon, such as Maker's Mark (optional)

1 crisp red apple

Place the apple cider, peppercorns, one of the cinnamon sticks, the cloves, and the star anise in a medium saucepan. Cut a large (1 × 4-inch) peel from the orange using a vegetable peeler and add it to the pan. Bring the cider mixture to a boil, lower the heat, and simmer for 5 minutes. Strain into a 4-cup glass measuring cup and discard the solids.

Pour the hot cider into mugs or heatproof glasses. Add 2 tablespoons bourbon, if using, to each mug. Cut the orange in half through the stem, slice crosswise in ¼-inch-thick half-rounds, and add one slice to each mug. Cut the apple in half through the stem, remove the core, slice crosswise in ¼-inch-thick half-rounds, and add one slice to each glass. Serve hot with a cinnamon stick in each glass for stirring.

ultimate bloody marys

We've all had Bloody Marys and they're usually pretty good. But I set out to make the ultimate Bloody Mary by adding wasabi, chipotle pepper, lime zest, and Old Bay seasoning. The Sacramento tomato juice is sweet and the clam juice is briny. Served with stuffed olives and jumbo shrimp, this is like a meal in a glass!

MAKES 6 DRINKS

3 cups Sacramento tomato juice

2 (8-ounce) bottles clam juice, such as Bumble Bee

½ teaspoon grated lime zest

½ cup freshly squeezed lime juice (3 to 4 limes)

2 teaspoons wasabi powder

2 teaspoons Tabasco Chipotle Pepper Sauce (see note)

1 tablespoon Worcestershire sauce

1 cup good vodka, such as Grey Goose

Kosher salt and freshly ground black pepper

2 tablespoons Old Bay Seasoning

7 lime wedges, divided

18 large pimento-stuffed olives, such as Sable & Rosenfeld

6 cooked and peeled jumbo shrimp, with tails on

In a large pitcher, stir together the tomato juice, clam juice, and lime zest. In a small glass measuring cup, whisk together the lime juice and wasabi powder, then add to the pitcher. Stir in the Tabasco, Worcestershire, vodka, 1 teaspoon salt, and ½ teaspoon pepper.

Spread the Old Bay Seasoning on a small plate. Moisten the rims of six highball glasses by running a lime wedge around the edge of each glass and dip the rims in the Old Bay Seasoning. Set aside to dry.

Fill the glasses half full with ice and pour in the Bloody Mary mixture. For each drink, add 2 or 3 olives and a lime wedge threaded on a 6-inch skewer, then place one shrimp on the rim of each glass. Serve cold.

Tabasco Chipotle Pepper Sauce is sold in grocery stores next to the Tabasco sauce.

make ahead: *You can make the Bloody Mary mixture up to an hour ahead; more than that and the spices become too strong.*

frozen palomas

I originally wrote a recipe for Palomas, which are like Margaritas but made with freshly squeezed grapefruit juice. Then, Jeffrey and I went to Wilson, Wyoming, to visit friends and they took us to a fabulous food store called Basecamp, which makes frozen drinks, including frozen Palomas. After that trip, I decided to serve my drink frozen, too. These are so refreshing on a hot summer night.

MAKES 4 DRINKS

1½ cups freshly squeezed ruby red grapefruit juice (3 to 4 grapefruit)

1 cup white tequila, such as Casamigos

½ cup freshly squeezed lime juice (3 to 4 limes)

¼ cup simple syrup (see note)

2 cups ice

Kosher salt

4 thin wedges ruby red grapefruit, for garnish

For simple syrup, combine 1 cup sugar and 1 cup water in a small pot and heat just until the sugar dissolves and the mixture is clear. Refrigerate until cold.

Combine the grapefruit juice, tequila, lime juice, and simple syrup in a quart container and freeze it for at least 6 hours (or overnight), until solid. Break up the mixture with a fork and transfer half of it to the jar of a blender. Add 1 cup of the ice and ⅛ teaspoon salt and blend until smooth. Divide the frozen mixture between two highball glasses, then repeat with the remaining mixture, ice, and salt. Garnish each glass with a grapefruit wedge and serve frozen.

pomegranate gimlets

What is it about drinking a cocktail in a martini glass that makes us feel so glamorous—like Cary Grant and Grace Kelly? This delicious gimlet was made for me by my friends Rob Marshall and John DeLuca. They updated the classic cocktail with pomegranate juice and of course served it in frozen martini glasses because they really are glamorous.

MAKES 6 DRINKS

1½ cups gin, such as Tanqueray

1 cup pomegranate juice,
such as Pom Wonderful

1 cup freshly squeezed lime juice
(6 to 8 limes)

½ cup simple syrup
(note page 35)

Pomegranate seeds, for garnish

6 lime slices, for garnish

At least one hour before serving, place six martini glasses in the freezer.

Combine the gin, pomegranate juice, lime juice, and simple syrup in a large pitcher. Fill a cocktail shaker half full with ice and add the drink mixture until the shaker is three quarters full. Shake for a full 15 seconds (it's longer than you think!). Pour the mixture into the frozen martini glasses and garnish with a teaspoon of pomegranate seeds and a slice of lime. Repeat with the remaining drink mixture and serve ice cold.

potato galettes with smoked salmon

When Jeffrey and I were in L.A., our friend Nancy Meyers invited us over for cocktails (yes, her gorgeous house actually does look like a Nancy Meyers movie). Nancy asked her friend and caterer Jennifer Naylor to send over her famous potato galette with smoked salmon. Yum! My version has warm, crunchy potatoes that are spread with cold crème fraîche and topped with briny smoked salmon.

MAKES 2 GALETTES /
SERVES 6

2 large russet baking potatoes
(1¼ pounds total)

Kosher salt and freshly ground
black pepper

Canola oil

4 tablespoons (½ stick) unsalted
butter, melted

4 tablespoons crème fraîche

¼ pound thinly sliced smoked
salmon, preferably Scottish

Minced fresh chives, for serving

make ahead: *Prepare the potato galettes up to an hour ahead and reheat directly on an oven rack in a 400-degree oven for 5 to 10 minutes, until heated through. Assemble just before serving.*

Peel the potatoes, then cut them lengthwise in long matchsticks, using the finest julienne blade of a mandoline. Spread the potatoes out neatly in one layer on a clean kitchen towel or paper towels, roll the towel up, and squeeze lightly to dry the potatoes without breaking them up. Put the potatoes into a bowl and toss them with 1 teaspoon salt and ½ teaspoon pepper.

Heat 2 tablespoons oil in a small (8-inch) omelet pan (a sauté pan with sloped sides) over medium heat. Add half of the potatoes to the pan and press lightly with a large metal spatula to make the shreds lie flat. Cook them undisturbed for 5 minutes. Drizzle one tablespoon of the butter around the edge of the pan and cook the potatoes for another 3 to 5 minutes, until nicely browned on the bottom. Loosen the galette gently around the edge with the metal spatula and flip it over. (Be careful! The oil and butter underneath are very hot!) Add another tablespoon of butter around the edge and cook the galette for 4 to 5 minutes longer, until the second side is nicely browned. With the metal spatula, transfer the galette to a paper towel–lined plate and set aside. Repeat with the rest of the potatoes and butter to make a second galette.

Place the two galettes on a cutting board. Spread each galette with 2 tablespoons of the crème fraîche and a layer of smoked salmon, covering the galette completely. Sprinkle with minced chives and sprinkle lightly with salt. Use a large chef's knife to cut each galette into 6 wedges and serve hot.

fig & cheese toasts

Jeffrey and I were having some friends for drinks and he couldn't believe how quickly I put these appetizers together! You put the fig spread on toast, then add some creamy cheese, sprinkle with microgreens, and drizzle it all with syrupy balsamic vinegar. They taste like grown-up cream cheese and jelly sandwiches.

SERVES 6 TO 8

1 (1-pound) loaf country bread, halved, and sliced crosswise ⅜ inch thick

1 (8.5-ounce) jar good fig spread, such as Dalmatia (see note)

8 ounces plain creamy cheese, such as goat cheese or cream cheese

Kosher salt and freshly ground black pepper

2 ripe fresh figs, halved and thinly sliced lengthwise

Microgreens

Syrupy balsamic vinegar

I prefer fig spread, which has less sugar than fig jam or fig preserves, but of course you can use either. Choose a fig spread that is quite thick or it will be hard to spread the cheese on top.

Toast the bread in a toaster and while still warm, spread the fig spread on each slice to cover it entirely. Place the cheese in a bowl and heat in the microwave for 30 to 45 seconds, until it's creamy and spreadable. Spread a layer of the cheese on the fig spread, leaving the edges of the fig spread visible. Sprinkle lightly with salt and pepper. Cut each toast crosswise to make appetizers that will be easy to eat. Lightly drizzle each piece with the balsamic vinegar, and top with a few microgreens. Serve at room temperature.

warm spinach & artichoke dip

I'm old enough to remember spinach and artichoke dip from the 1970s but there are a million bad versions around. When it's good, it can be delicious. My updated spinach and artichoke dip has caramelized onion and chopped artichoke hearts; it's crusty around the edges and creamy in the middle. I serve it with toasted slices of a crusty baguette.

SERVES 8 TO 10

2 large yellow onions

4 tablespoons (½ stick) unsalted butter

¼ cup good olive oil

¼ teaspoon ground cayenne pepper

Kosher salt and freshly ground black pepper

1 tablespoon minced garlic (3 cloves)

4 ounces cream cheese, at room temperature

½ cup sour cream

½ cup good mayonnaise, such as Hellmann's

1 (9-ounce) package frozen artichoke hearts, defrosted

1 (10-ounce) package frozen chopped spinach, defrosted

1¼ cups freshly grated Italian Parmesan cheese, divided

1 baguette, sliced diagonally ½ inch thick, toasted, for serving

make ahead: *Assemble the dish, cover, and refrigerate for up to a day. Bake before serving.*

Preheat the oven to 400 degrees.

Cut the onions in half through the stem, then slice them in ⅛-inch-thick half-rounds. (You will have about 3 cups of onions.) In a large (12-inch) sauté pan, heat the butter and oil over medium heat. Add the onions, cayenne pepper, 1 teaspoon salt, and ½ teaspoon black pepper, and sauté for 10 minutes. Reduce the heat to medium-low and sauté, stirring occasionally, for 20 minutes, until the onions are browned and caramelized. Stir in the garlic and cook for one minute.

Meanwhile, place the cream cheese, sour cream, and mayonnaise in the bowl of an electric mixer fitted with the paddle attachment and beat until smooth. Lightly squeeze the liquid out of the artichoke hearts, chop roughly, and add to the bowl. Lightly squeeze the liquid out of the spinach and add to the bowl. Add the onion mixture and stir to combine. Stir in ¾ cup of the Parmesan, 1 teaspoon salt, and ½ teaspoon black pepper, and transfer to an 11 × 8 × 1½ -inch oval baking dish. Sprinkle on the remaining ½ cup of Parmesan. Bake for 20 to 25 minutes, until the edges are browned and bubbly. Serve warm with slices of baguette for scooping.

fresh crab nachos

When we were testing these, my assistant Kristina remarked, "If you serve these when the football game is on, no one's going to watch the game!" These nachos are seriously that good—layers of chips, fresh crab, chiles, Cheddar, pickled jalapeños, avocados, and tomatoes. They're crunchy, spicy, and cheesy and perfect for sharing.

SERVES 8

6 ounces cream cheese, at room temperature

½ cup good mayonnaise, such as Hellmann's

¼ cup sour cream

12 ounces fresh jumbo lump crabmeat (see note)

¾ cup minced scallions, white and green parts (4 to 5 scallions)

1 (4-ounce) can diced green chiles, such as Goya

Grated zest of 1 lime

Kosher salt and freshly ground black pepper

12 ounces sturdy yellow corn chips, such as Garden of Eatin'

6 ounces freshly grated extra-sharp white Cheddar

6 ounces freshly grated Monterey Jack

4 ounces canned pickled jalapeño pepper slices, drained

5 large plum tomatoes, seeded, cored, and small-diced

1 cup minced yellow onion

3 tablespoons minced fresh jalapeño pepper, seeds removed

2 tablespoons freshly squeezed lime juice

1 tablespoon good olive oil

1 large ripe Hass avocado, pitted, peeled, and ⅓-inch diced

3 tablespoons minced fresh parsley or cilantro

Juice of ½ lime, for serving

I prefer jumbo lump crabmeat instead of shredded because you can really taste the crabmeat.

Pick through the crabmeat to remove any shells.

Be sure to wash your hands after handling the chiles and pickled jalapeños so you don't get the spicy oils in your eyes.

Preheat the oven to 375 degrees.

In a medium bowl, stir together the cream cheese, mayonnaise, and sour cream until smooth. Gently stir in the crabmeat, scallions, chiles, lime zest, 2 teaspoons salt, and 1 teaspoon black pepper and set aside.

Distribute half of the corn chips on a large (12 × 18 × 2-inch) ovenproof serving platter (or a sheet pan). Spoon half of the crab mixture over the chips in dollops and then sprinkle with half of the Cheddar, half of the Monterey Jack, and all of the pickled jalapeños. Sprinkle with the remaining chips, then distribute the remaining crab mixture and cheeses on top. Bake for 20 to 30 minutes, until the cheese is melted and bubbling.

Meanwhile, prepare the topping. In a large bowl, combine the tomatoes, onion, jalapeño pepper, lime juice, olive oil, avocado, parsley, and 1 teaspoon salt. Spoon onto the nachos, sprinkle with lime juice, and serve hot.

cacio e pepe cheese puffs

One of my favorite restaurants is Missy Robbins's Lilia in Brooklyn. The food is very earthy but with incredible layers of sophisticated flavor. The first time we went there, we ordered huge cheese puffs filled with Pecorino cheese and black pepper. I came right home and made these appetizers, which are inspired by Lilia's puffs.

MAKES 35 TO 40 PUFFS

1 cup whole milk

¼ pound (1 stick) unsalted butter

Kosher salt and freshly ground black pepper

1 cup all-purpose flour

4 extra-large eggs

½ cup freshly ground aged Italian Pecorino cheese, plus extra for sprinkling (see note)

½ cup freshly ground Italian Parmesan cheese

1 extra-large egg beaten with 1 teaspoon water or milk, for egg wash

Normally I grind rather than grate hard cheeses, such as Pecorino and Parmesan, in the food processor for consistency in measuring.

To scald milk, heat it to just below the boiling point, when bubbles start to form around the perimeter. Don't allow it to boil.

make ahead: *Bake the puffs, allow them to cool, and freeze in a sealed bag. Place on a sheet pan lined with parchment paper and reheat at 375 degrees for 10 minutes.*

Preheat the oven to 425 degrees. Arrange two racks evenly spaced in the oven.

In a medium (4½-inch-diameter × 6-inch-high) saucepan, heat the milk, butter, 1 teaspoon salt, and 1 teaspoon pepper over medium heat, just until the milk is scalded (see note). Add the flour all at once and beat it vigorously with a wooden spoon until the mixture comes together. Lower the heat and cook, stirring constantly, for 2 minutes. Dump the mixture into the bowl of a food processor fitted with the steel blade. Immediately add the eggs, ½ cup of Pecorino, and the Parmesan and pulse until the eggs and cheeses are completely incorporated.

Working in batches, spoon the mixture into a large pastry bag fitted with a plain ⅝-inch round pastry tip. Pipe the dough in mounds 1¼ inches wide and ¾ inch high (1 inch apart) on two sheet pans lined with parchment paper. (They should look like huge Hershey's Kisses.) With a wet finger, lightly press down the swirl on top of each puff. (You can also use two spoons to scoop the mixture and shape the puffs.) Brush the top of each puff lightly with the egg wash and sprinkle with Pecorino, salt, and pepper. Bake for 15 to 20 minutes, until browned. Rotate the pans halfway through so they brown evenly. Serve hot.

grilled oysters with lemon dill butter

I have to admit, I'm not the biggest fan of the slippery texture of raw oysters but I do love their briny flavor. My solution is to cook them ever so slightly on the grill with lots of melted butter, lemon, dill, and garlic. They're not really "cooked," but they're also not raw so you get the best flavor from the oysters and the richness and acidity from the lemon butter. Now, that's comfort food!

SERVES 6

¼ pound (1 stick) unsalted butter, at room temperature

1 teaspoon minced garlic

1 teaspoon minced fresh dill

1 teaspoon grated lemon zest

1 tablespoon freshly squeezed lemon juice

Kosher salt and freshly ground black pepper

24 large fresh oysters, shucked and on the half shell (see note)

Sea salt or fleur de sel

Have your fish store open the oysters and leave them on the bottom rounded shell. Keep refrigerated and use as soon as possible after they're opened.

Heat a charcoal or gas grill. If using charcoal, make sure you have a full layer of hot coals on the grate.

Meanwhile, in the bowl of an electric mixer fitted with the paddle attachment, combine the butter, garlic, dill, lemon zest, lemon juice, 1 teaspoon kosher salt, and ¼ teaspoon pepper and beat on medium speed until just combined.

Place the oysters on the half shell on a sheet pan. Place 1 level teaspoon of the herbed butter on each oyster (you'll have just enough butter for all the oysters). Place slightly crumpled sheets of aluminum foil on the grill grates to keep the oysters stable. Transfer the oysters to the foil, making sure the shells are level so the butter doesn't spill out. Cover the grill with the lid, making sure the vents are open, and cook for 2 to 3 minutes, until the butter comes to a simmer and the oysters are just heated through. Transfer carefully to a platter, sprinkle with sea salt, and serve hot.

spicy pimento cheese spread

Pimento cheese spread definitely qualifies as comfort food. Mine is an update with ingredients like good sharp Cheddar, pickled jalapeños, and Sriracha. This recipe is inspired by the pimento cheese from a Brooklyn cheese shop that I love called Stinky (what a great name!).

SERVES 8

8 ounces cream cheese, at room temperature

¾ cup good mayonnaise, such as Hellmann's

1½ teaspoons granulated onion (not onion powder)

2 large garlic cloves, grated (see note)

1 teaspoon whole celery seed

Kosher salt

¾ cup canned pickled jalapeño peppers, drained and chopped

½ cup chopped scallions, white and green parts (3 to 4 scallions)

½ cup chopped roasted red peppers, drained (4 ounces)

4 cups grated sharp white Cheddar, such as 2-year aged Grafton (10 ounces)

1 tablespoon Sriracha

Ritz crackers, corn chips, and/or crudités, for serving

In a large bowl, combine the cream cheese, mayonnaise, onion, garlic, celery seed, and ½ teaspoon salt with a wooden spoon. Add the jalapeños, scallions, red peppers, Cheddar, and Sriracha and combine well. Taste for seasonings and serve with crackers, corn chips, and/or crudités.

Grate the garlic on a rasp, the way you'd grate lemon zest. The Cheddar is best grated on the side of a box grater, the way you'd grate carrots.

kielbasa with mustard dip

Sometimes you just need an appetizer fast! Friends were stopping by and I hadn't planned a thing to serve so I went to the fridge and found some really good kielbasa sausage. I sliced it, seared it in a pan, and served it—right from the pan—with a good mustard dip. They loved it!

SERVES 6 TO 8

1¼ pounds smoked kielbasa
(Polish sausage)

Good olive oil

½ cup good mayonnaise,
such as Hellmann's

2 tablespoons Dijon mustard

1 teaspoon whole-grain mustard

1 teaspoon prepared horseradish

Kosher salt and freshly ground
black pepper

Slice the kielbasa crosswise ½ inch thick diagonally. Heat 2 tablespoons olive oil in a medium (10 to 11-inch) sauté pan, add the kielbasa, and cook over medium-high heat for 5 to 6 minutes, turning occasionally, until the kielbasa is nicely browned on both sides.

Meanwhile, in a medium bowl, whisk together the mayonnaise, Dijon mustard, whole-grain mustard, horseradish, ½ teaspoon salt, and ¼ teaspoon pepper. Serve the kielbasa hot from the pan with small wooden skewers and a dish of the mustard sauce on the side for dipping.

lunch

chicken pot pie soup

—

split pea soup with crispy kielbasa

—

baked fish chowder

—

maine lobster stew

—

salmorejo

—

fresh pea salad with mint & manchego

—

seared tuna & avocado rolls

—

ultimate tuna melts

—

lobster blts

—

creamy tomato bisque

—

cheddar & chutney grilled cheese

—

baked raclette

—

broccoli & kale salad

—

tomato & goat cheese crostata

—

finding inspiration

People ask me all the time how I get inspired. The truth is, after writing twelve cookbooks, it's not always easy to think of new ideas, so I look for inspiration everywhere. A dish I order in a restaurant or specialty food store might intrigue me. I love to cruise grocery stores and farmers' markets looking for new ingredients like shishito peppers, fig spread, or truffle butter. In the past few years, social media has also become one of my biggest sources of inspiration; it's not uncommon for me to see something on Instagram that gets me running to the kitchen.

One of the people in the food world who inspires me most is my friend Eli Zabar, who owns specialty food stores and restaurants in New York City. It's not only his creative ideas but also his constant curiosity. He's always asking people what they do with everything—the raspberry guy at the street market in Paris and the farmer who grows heirloom tomatoes on the roof of his building. Eli's food is exactly what I love: good home-style cooking rather than restaurant food, but made with

really good ingredients and prepared in a modern way. In fact, when Food Network once asked me to list my three all-time favorite dishes for their show *The Best Thing I Ever Ate,* the grilled cheese sandwiches and tomato soup at Eli's restaurant E.A.T. were on my list. They inspired my recipes for Cheddar & Chutney Grilled Cheese (page 84) and Creamy Tomato Bisque (page 83). It's the simplest, most familiar lunch, but so much better than you expect.

Sometimes recipes end up in a book through a chain of events. The Broccoli & Kale Salad (page 91) is a dish I first had for lunch at Jean-Georges Vongerichten's restaurant Topping Rose House in Bridgehampton, New York. I loved it so much that I came right home and made my own version. The salad was so simple and beautiful—bright green kale and broccoli with a jammy soft-cooked egg on top—that I snapped a picture and posted it on Instagram. The post got so many positive comments that I knew I had to include the recipe in this book! I hope you'll find lots of inspiration from my Instagram (below), as well, so you can make dishes that your family and friends will love!

chicken pot pie soup

This was a little crazy: I was walking through an airport once and spotted chicken pot pie soup on a restaurant menu. What a good idea! It was actually harder to make than it sounded—my first few attempts just tasted like chicken pot pie filling, not soup. This one, though, hit all the right comforting notes, with good chicken stock, roasted chicken, and puff pastry croutons.

SERVES 6

3 chicken breasts, skin-on,
bone-in (2½ to 3 pounds total)

Good olive oil

Kosher salt and freshly ground
black pepper

6 tablespoons (¾ stick)
unsalted butter

5 cups chopped leeks,
white and light green parts
(3 leeks) (see note)

4 cups chopped fennel, tops
and cores removed (2 bulbs)

3 cups (½-inch) diced scrubbed
carrots (5 medium)

1 tablespoon minced garlic
(3 cloves)

1 tablespoon chopped fresh
tarragon leaves

¼ cup Wondra flour

¾ cup cream sherry, divided

7 cups good chicken stock,
preferably homemade
(see page 64)

1 (2 × 3-inch) piece of Italian
Parmesan cheese rind

1 (10-ounce) box frozen peas

1 cup frozen whole pearl onions

¼ cup minced fresh parsley

Puff Pastry Croutons
(recipe follows)

Preheat the oven to 350 degrees.

Place the chicken on a sheet pan skin side up, rub the skin with olive oil, and season generously with salt and pepper. Roast for 35 minutes, until a thermometer registers 130 to 140 degrees. Set aside until cool enough to handle. Remove and discard the skin and bones and cut the chicken in 1-inch dice. Set aside.

Meanwhile, melt the butter in a medium (10 to 11-inch) heavy-bottomed pot or Dutch oven, such as Le Creuset, over medium heat. Add the leeks, fennel, and carrots, and sauté over medium-high heat for 10 minutes, stirring occasionally, until the leeks are tender but not browned. Stir in the garlic and tarragon and cook for one minute. Sprinkle on the flour and cook, stirring constantly, for 2 minutes. Add ½ cup of the sherry, the chicken stock, 4 teaspoons salt, 1½ teaspoons pepper, and the Parmesan rind. Bring to a boil, lower the heat, and simmer, partially covered, for 20 minutes.

Add the chicken, peas, and onions and simmer uncovered for 5 minutes. Off the heat, remove the Parmesan rind and add the remaining ¼ cup of sherry and the parsley. Serve hot in large shallow bowls with two Puff Pastry Croutons on top.

To prep the leeks, cut off the dark green leaves at a 45-degree angle and discard. Chop the white and light green parts, wash well in a bowl of water, and spin dry in a salad spinner. Wet leeks will steam rather than sauté.

puff pastry croutons

MAKES 12 CROUTONS

All-purpose flour

1 sheet of frozen puff pastry, such as Pepperidge Farm, defrosted (see note)

1 extra-large egg beaten with 1 tablespoon heavy cream, for egg wash

Kosher salt and freshly ground black pepper

Preheat the oven to 400 degrees. Line a sheet pan with parchment paper.

Lightly dust a board and rolling pin with flour. Unfold the sheet of puff pastry on the board, dust it lightly with flour, and lightly roll the pastry just to smooth out the folds.

With star-shaped or fluted round cookie cutters, cut 12 stars or rounds of pastry and place them on the prepared sheet pan. Brush the tops with the egg wash, sprinkle with salt and pepper, and bake for 8 to 10 minutes, until puffed and golden brown.

Defrost puff pastry overnight in the refrigerator. You want the pastry to be very cold when you bake it.

make ahead: *Prepare the pastry cutouts and refrigerate. Bake just before serving.*

split pea soup with crispy kielbasa

One of my all-time favorite comfort foods is a bowl of split pea soup, dating back to the days when my mother served us canned pea soup with cut-up hot dogs (very '50s!). Now I prefer a big pot of homemade soup to serve with sautéed kielbasa on top. I love the way the earthy, creamy soup contrasts with the crispy, spicy sausage.

SERVES 6

Good olive oil

2 cups chopped leeks,
white and light green parts,
spun-dried (2 leeks)

1½ cups chopped yellow onion
(1 large)

2 cups (½-inch) diced, scrubbed
carrots (3 large)

1 tablespoon minced garlic
(3 cloves)

1 pound dry green split peas

8 cups good chicken stock,
preferably homemade
(recipe follows)

1 smoked ham hock

8 fresh thyme sprigs, tied with
kitchen twine

2 large fresh bay leaves

Kosher salt and freshly ground
black pepper

12 ounces smoked kielbasa, halved
lengthwise and sliced diagonally
in ¼-inch-thick pieces

Minced fresh parsley,
for serving

make ahead: *Reheat the soup over low heat, adding chicken stock or water to thin.*

Heat ¼ cup olive oil in a large (11 to 12-inch) pot or Dutch oven, such as Le Creuset, over medium-high heat. Add the leeks, onion, and carrots and cook for 7 to 8 minutes, stirring occasionally, until tender and starting to brown. Stir in the garlic and cook for one minute. Stir in the peas to coat with oil and cook for one minute. Add 8 cups of the chicken stock, 2 cups water, the ham hock, thyme bundle, bay leaves, 2 teaspoons salt, and 1 teaspoon pepper. Bring to a boil, lower the heat, and simmer, partially covered, for 1¼ hours, stirring occasionally, until the peas are very tender and falling apart. After 45 minutes, stir more frequently, scraping the bottom of the pot to be sure the soup doesn't burn.

Discard the thyme bundle, bay leaves, and ham hock. Transfer 2 cups of the soup to the bowl of a food processor fitted with the steel blade and purée. Return the purée to the pot, adding more chicken stock or water if the soup is too thick.

To serve, heat 2 tablespoons olive oil in a medium (10 to 11-inch) sauté pan over medium heat. Add the kielbasa and sauté for 5 to 6 minutes, tossing occasionally, until the kielbasa is browned. Serve the soup hot with the kielbasa and parsley sprinkled on top.

homemade chicken stock

I think of homemade chicken stock as liquid gold. Nothing available on the market has the depth of flavor or richness of homemade stock. It gives anything you make with it such great body and aroma. Just having a big pot of chicken stock simmering away on my stove makes me feel good.

MAKES 5 TO 6 QUARTS

3 (5-pound) roasting chickens

3 large yellow onions, unpeeled and quartered

6 carrots, unpeeled and halved

4 celery stalks with leaves, cut into thirds

4 parsnips, unpeeled and cut in half

20 sprigs fresh parsley

15 sprigs fresh thyme

20 sprigs fresh dill

1 head garlic, unpeeled and cut in half crosswise

2 tablespoons kosher salt

2 teaspoons whole black peppercorns

Place the chickens, onions, carrots, celery, parsnips, parsley, thyme, dill, garlic, salt, and peppercorns in a 16 to 20-quart stockpot. Add 7 quarts of water and bring to a boil. Lower the heat and simmer uncovered for 4 hours. Allow the stock to cool for 30 minutes. Strain the contents of the pot through a colander into a large bowl and discard the solids. Pack the stock in containers and refrigerate for up to a few days or freeze for up to 6 months.

baked fish chowder

On a cold winter night, I love to make a big batch of soup like this fish chowder. It's made with onions, bacon, white wine, saffron, and a touch of Pernod, the anise-flavored liqueur that's often used in bouillabaisse. This soup is rich and so delicious!

SERVES 4 TO 6

½ pound thick-cut applewood-smoked bacon, ¾-inch diced (see note)

6 cups yellow onions, halved and thinly sliced crosswise (3 large)

3 cups (½-inch) diced celery (6 large stalks)

1 tablespoon fresh thyme leaves

¾ cup good dry white wine, such as Chablis

Kosher salt and freshly ground black pepper

1 pound (2-inch diameter) Yukon Gold potatoes, peeled, sliced ¼ inch thick

4 tablespoons (½ stick) unsalted butter, diced

4 cups seafood stock, heated to a simmer (see note)

¾ teaspoon saffron threads

2 pounds fresh skinless cod fillets

½ cup half-and-half

½ cup heavy cream

2 tablespoons Pernod liqueur

Minced fresh parsley

Preheat the oven to 350 degrees.

Place the bacon in a medium (10 to 11-inch) pot or Dutch oven, such as Le Creuset, over medium-low heat and cook for 10 minutes, stirring occasionally, until browned and crisp. With a slotted spoon, transfer the bacon to a plate and set aside. Add the onions, celery, and thyme to the bacon fat and sauté for 10 to 12 minutes, stirring occasionally, until the vegetables are tender and beginning to brown. Add the wine, 2 teaspoons salt, and 1 teaspoon pepper, scraping up the brown bits in the pot. Simmer for 2 minutes.

Transfer half of the onion mixture to a bowl and spread the remaining onions in the pot. Distribute half of the potatoes on the onions, then half of the butter. Spread the reserved onion mixture on top, then the remaining potatoes and butter. Add the stock and saffron, cover the pot, and bake for 30 to 40 minutes, until the potatoes are almost tender when tested with a knife. (Leave the oven on.)

Cut the fish in very large (1 × 3-inch) chunks and sprinkle with 1 tablespoon salt and 1½ teaspoons pepper. Stir the half-and-half and cream into the pot and add the fish, pressing it into the liquid.

Cover and bake for 20 to 30 minutes, until the potatoes are done and the fish flakes easily. Add the bacon and Pernod, stirring very gently to avoid breaking up the fish, then cover and allow it to sit for 5 minutes. Ladle into large shallow bowls, sprinkle with parsley, and serve hot.

Nodine's makes the best thick-cut applewood-smoked bacon.

Your fish market probably makes a good seafood stock. Otherwise, use two (15-ounce) cans of Bar Harbor Seafood Stock.

maine lobster stew

This is called lobster stew in Maine; it's a rich lobster soup. First, you steep the shells in milk, cream, sherry, and saffron overnight to extract the lobster flavor and the next day you cook the lobster in the base with tarragon and more sherry. This stew gets its deep flavor from both dry and cream sherry.

SERVES 6

4 cooked (1¼-pound) lobsters (see note)

½ pound (2 sticks) unsalted butter, divided

1 cup *dry* sherry

3 cups whole milk

3 cups heavy cream

2 teaspoons sweet paprika, plus extra for serving

¼ teaspoon saffron threads

Kosher salt and freshly ground black pepper

1 tablespoon minced fresh tarragon

⅓ cup *cream* sherry, such as Harveys Bristol Cream

1 (14.5-ounce) can diced tomatoes

Chopped fresh chives, for serving

I have my fish store cook the lobsters and then I shell them at home. To cook them yourself, put them in a large pot of boiling salted water and cook them until they reach an internal temperature of 140 degrees on an instant-read thermometer.

Working over a large bowl, remove the lobster meat from the shells, reserving all the juices and shells. Cut the meat in (¾ to 1-inch) chunks, place in a covered container and refrigerate.

Melt 1 stick of the butter in a large (11 to 12-inch) heavy-bottomed pot or Dutch oven, such as Le Creuset, over medium-high heat. Add the lobster shells and the juices to the pot and cook for 3 minutes, tossing the shells to coat them with butter. Add the *dry* sherry, bring it to a boil, and simmer for 6 minutes. Add the milk, cream, the 2 teaspoons of paprika, the saffron, 2 teaspoons salt, and 1 teaspoon pepper. Bring to a boil, reduce the heat, and simmer uncovered for 15 minutes. Set aside to cool for 30 minutes. Cover and refrigerate for 12 to 24 hours to allow the flavors to blend.

With the pot still covered, heat the milk and lobster shells over medium heat until the liquid simmers. Strain through a fine-mesh sieve into a bowl and set aside, discarding the shells. Place the pot on the stove (no need to wash it), add the remaining ¼ pound butter, and heat until the butter melts. Off the heat, add the lobster, tarragon, 1 teaspoon salt, and ½ teaspoon pepper and allow to sit for 3 minutes. Add the *cream* sherry and tomatoes and allow to sit for 5 minutes. Add the strained milk mixture plus 1 teaspoon salt and bring to a boil. Lower the heat and simmer for 5 minutes. Ladle into bowls, sprinkle with paprika and chives, and serve hot.

salmorejo

My friend Miguel Flores-Vianna introduced me to salmorejo, which is similar to gazpacho but puréed with bread to thicken it. It's the easiest summer soup with tomatoes, peppers, red onion, and garlic. I garnish it with crispy croutons, cherry tomatoes, basil, and a drizzle of olive oil.

SERVES 4 TO 6

2 pounds large ripe red tomatoes, cored and roughly chopped (see note)

1 heaping cup diced country white bread, crusts removed

1 Holland red bell pepper, cored, seeded, and large-diced

½ cup chopped red onion

3 large garlic cloves

½ cup tomato purée, such as passata di pomodoro

2 tablespoons good sherry vinegar

Kosher salt and freshly ground black pepper

¾ cup good olive oil, plus extra for serving

Toasted Croutons, for serving

Cherry tomatoes, halved, for serving

Julienned fresh basil leaves, for serving

Flaked sea salt, such as Maldon, for serving

As tomatoes are the main ingredient, try to use summer or farm stand tomatoes.

Place the chopped fresh tomatoes, bread, bell pepper, onion, and garlic in the bowl of a food processor fitted with the steel blade or in the jar of a blender and purée until you can only see tiny bits of tomato skins. Transfer the mixture to a large bowl and whisk in the tomato purée, vinegar, 2 teaspoons salt, and 1 teaspoon black pepper. Slowly whisk in the olive oil.

Cover and refrigerate the soup for *just* 2 hours to allow the flavors to blend. If you refrigerate the soup for more than 2 hours, the olive oil will congeal so if you want to prepare the soup ahead, make it without the olive oil, refrigerate, and whisk in the oil just before serving.

Serve cold in large, shallow bowls and top with the croutons, cherry tomatoes, basil leaves, flaked sea salt, and a drizzle of olive oil.

toasted croutons

This is a great way to use up leftover bread and adds a nice crunch to all kinds of soups and salads. They are so much fresher and more flavorful than packaged croutons.

MAKES 1 CUP CROUTONS

Good olive oil, such as Olio Santo

2½ ounces country white bread, crusts removed and ½-inch diced

Kosher salt and freshly ground black pepper

Pour 2 tablespoons of olive oil in a small (8-inch) sauté pan and heat over medium-high heat until hot but not smoking. Add the bread and sauté, tossing occasionally, for 4 to 5 minutes, until evenly browned. Sprinkle generously with salt and pepper.

fresh pea salad
with mint & manchego

In the spring when fresh peas and sugar snap peas are available, I love to make this salad. It hits all the right notes—lemon vinaigrette, fresh mint, and big shavings of Spanish Manchego cheese that make it really satisfying.

SERVES 5 OR 6

Kosher salt and freshly ground black pepper

2 cups freshly shelled green peas (2 pounds in the pod) (see note)

14 ounces sugar snap peas, strings removed, julienned lengthwise

⅔ cup julienned fresh mint leaves

6 tablespoons freshly squeezed lemon juice (2 to 3 lemons)

½ cup good olive oil

6 ounces Manchego cheese, shaved with a vegetable peeler

Fill a medium saucepan with water, add 1 tablespoon salt, and bring to a boil. Fill a large bowl with ice water. Add the green peas to the boiling water and cook for 3 to 4 minutes, depending on their size, until crisp-tender. Drain and immediately plunge the peas into the ice water to stop the cooking. Drain again and transfer to a serving bowl. Add the snap peas and mint.

In a small glass measuring cup, whisk together the lemon juice, olive oil, 1 teaspoon salt, and ½ teaspoon pepper. Pour enough lemon vinaigrette over the salad to lightly coat all the ingredients. Sprinkle with ½ teaspoon salt and ¼ teaspoon pepper and toss together. Add the cheese to the salad and toss lightly so as not to break it up. Sprinkle with pepper, taste for seasonings, and serve at room temperature or chilled.

If you buy peas that are already shelled, you'll need 10 ounces.

seared tuna & avocado rolls

Lobster rolls are delicious but predictable so instead, I decided to fill rolls with tuna and avocado. The tuna is quickly seared, then diced and mixed with avocado, lime, scallions, and jalapeño. It all goes into a toasted bun with pickled shallots and chipotle mayonnaise on top. So good!

SERVES 6

¾ pound sushi-grade tuna steak, sliced ¾ inch thick

Good olive oil

Kosher salt and freshly ground black pepper

Grated zest of 1 lime

3 tablespoons freshly squeezed lime juice

1½ teaspoons soy sauce

6 dashes Tabasco sauce

¼ cup minced scallions, white and green parts (2 scallions)

2 teaspoons minced fresh jalapeño pepper, seeds removed

1 ripe Hass avocado

1 shallot, halved lengthwise and thinly sliced crosswise

2 tablespoons good red wine vinegar

2 tablespoons unsalted butter

6 top-split hot dog buns, such as Pepperidge Farm

Chipotle Mayonnaise (recipe follows)

Heat a medium (10 to 11-inch) dry cast-iron skillet over high heat for 3 minutes. Brush the tuna all over with olive oil and sprinkle it generously with salt and black pepper. Sear the tuna in the skillet for exactly one minute on each side. (The inside will be raw.) Transfer to a cutting board, cut into ½ to ¾-inch dice, and set aside.

In a large bowl, combine ¼ cup olive oil, the lime zest, lime juice, soy sauce, Tabasco, 1½ teaspoons salt, and 1 teaspoon black pepper. Add the tuna, scallions, and jalapeño. Cut the avocado in half, remove the pit, peel, and cut ½ to ¾-inch dice. Carefully stir the avocado into the tuna mixture and set aside for 20 minutes.

Meanwhile, combine the shallot and vinegar in a small bowl and set aside.

Place the butter in a large (12-inch) sauté pan over medium-high heat and heat until the butter sizzles. Without opening the buns, toast them on each side for one minute, until nicely browned. Line the buns up on a platter, cut sides up, and spoon the tuna mixture into the buns. Drizzle with the Chipotle Mayonnaise and sprinkle on the pickled shallots. Serve while the buns are warm.

chipotle mayonnaise

MAKES ABOUT 1 CUP

1 cup good mayonnaise,
such as Hellmann's

1 canned chipotle pepper
in adobo sauce

2 teaspoons adobo sauce
(from the can of chipotles)

1 teaspoon freshly squeezed
lime juice

Kosher salt

Place the mayonnaise, chipotle pepper, adobo sauce, lime juice, and 1¼ teaspoons salt in the bowl of a food processor fitted with the steel blade. Process until smooth. Refrigerate for up to a week.

ultimate tuna melts

When I asked friends to name their favorite comfort food, so many said a tuna fish sandwich! I've made a Barefoot Contessa version of a tuna melt with good Spanish tuna packed in oil, fresh scallions, dill, and nutty Swiss cheese plus a sprinkling of microgreens on top. This is no ordinary tuna sandwich!

SERVES 4

2 (6 to 8-ounce) jars imported tuna packed in olive oil, drained

½ cup (¼-inch) diced hearts of celery

½ cup minced scallions, white and light green parts (3 scallions)

3 tablespoons minced fresh dill

2 tablespoons freshly squeezed lemon juice

Kosher salt and freshly ground black pepper

¾ cup good mayonnaise, such as Hellmann's

1 teaspoon anchovy paste (optional)

4 large slices bread, such as Pepperidge Farm Farmhouse Hearty White

4 ounces Swiss cheese, such as Emmentaler, grated

1 ounce microgreens

In a medium bowl, flake the tuna finely with a fork. Add the celery, scallions, and dill, and continue mixing and fluffing with the fork until combined. Add the lemon juice, 1½ teaspoons salt, and ¾ teaspoon pepper. Combine the mayonnaise and anchovy paste, if using, and mix into the tuna.

Preheat the broiler. Toast the bread in a toaster and place the slices in a single layer on a sheet pan. Spread a quarter of the tuna mixture thickly and evenly on each piece of bread, covering the entire slice. Sprinkle the cheese evenly on the 4 sandwiches, covering the tuna completely. Broil for 1 to 2 minutes, just until the cheese melts and starts to brown. (Watch it carefully!) Sprinkle with the microgreens and serve hot.

I use Ortiz line-caught tuna packed in oil.

lobster blts

I'm always looking for a way to update classic recipes, such as my favorite BLTs. If you start with really good ingredients, you can make something delicious but if you add lobster and avocado, you have a classic sandwich that's good enough to serve your mother-in-law!

MAKES 4 SANDWICHES

4 slices thick-cut applewood-smoked bacon, such as Nodine's

½ cup good mayonnaise, such as Hellmann's

¼ cup ketchup, such as Heinz

1 tablespoon sweet relish

Kosher salt and freshly ground black pepper

2 ripe Hass avocados, pitted and peeled

Juice of 1 lemon

8 (½-inch-thick) slices good bakery white bread, lightly toasted (see note)

4 large Bibb, Boston, or butter lettuce leaves

4 (¼-inch-thick) ripe red tomato slices (1 large tomato)

½ pound cooked lobster meat, sliced (see note)

To toast the bread in the oven, arrange the slices on a sheet pan and place in a preheated 400 degree oven for 10 minutes, until lightly toasted.

If you buy cooked lobsters, two (1¼-pound) lobsters will yield ½ pound of lobster meat.

Preheat the oven to 400 degrees. Place a baking rack on a sheet pan and lay the bacon on the rack in a single layer. Roast the bacon for 15 to 20 minutes, until browned. Transfer to a plate lined with paper towels and set aside.

Meanwhile, for the dressing, whisk together the mayonnaise, ketchup, relish, ¼ teaspoon salt, and ⅛ teaspoon pepper in a medium bowl and set aside. Slice the avocados crosswise ¼ inch thick, place the slices in a bowl with the lemon juice, toss gently, and set aside.

To assemble, place 4 slices of toast on a board and slather them generously with the dressing. On each sandwich, place first a lettuce leaf, then a layer of avocado, then a slice of tomato. Sprinkle generously with salt and pepper. Cut a slice of bacon in half and place both halves on the tomato. Top with a quarter of the lobster. Generously spread more sauce on the remaining 4 slices of toast and place them, sauce side down, on the sandwiches. Serve immediately.

creamy tomato bisque

Isn't a steaming bowl of tomato soup the ultimate comfort food? While heating up a can of tomato soup may do in a pinch, the real thing is so much better—with slowly sautéed onions and leeks plus good Italian tomatoes and a hint of saffron. You'll never go back to that can again!

SERVES 8

3 tablespoons unsalted butter

Good olive oil

1½ cups chopped yellow onion (1 large)

¾ cup chopped shallots (2 large)

1 cup chopped leek, white and light green parts, spun-dried

3 (28-ounce) cans crushed tomatoes, preferably San Marzano

4 cups whole milk

2 cups heavy cream

½ teaspoon saffron threads

¼ teaspoon crushed red pepper flakes

Kosher salt and freshly ground black pepper

Grated Italian Parmesan cheese, for garnish

Minced fresh parsley, for garnish

make ahead: *Prepare the soup completely and refrigerate. Reheat over medium-low heat, adding milk or water as needed to make the soup the desired consistency.*

Heat the butter and 1 tablespoon olive oil in a large (11 to 12-inch) pot or Dutch oven, such as Le Creuset, over medium-low heat. Add the onion, shallots, and leek, and sauté for 8 to 10 minutes, stirring occasionally, until the vegetables are tender. Add the tomatoes, milk, cream, saffron, red pepper flakes, 1 tablespoon salt, and 1½ teaspoons black pepper. Raise the heat, bring to a boil, then lower the heat and simmer uncovered for 30 to 40 minutes, stirring occasionally, until the flavors are blended and the soup is slightly thickened.

Off the heat, stir in 1 teaspoon salt and ½ teaspoon black pepper. Serve hot, sprinkled with the Parmesan and parsley.

cheddar & chutney grilled cheese

Isn't a really good grilled cheese sandwich the ultimate comfort food? This isn't Wonder Bread with some mystery cheese inside—it's bakery white bread piled high with extra-sharp Cheddar and savory chutney to brighten the flavor. A bowl of Creamy Tomato Bisque (page 83) to go with it wouldn't hurt either.

MAKES 6 SANDWICHES

12 (¼-inch-thick) slices good bakery white bread

¼ pound (1 stick) unsalted butter, melted

1 (8.5-ounce) jar mango chutney, such as Stonewall Kitchen

3 cups grated extra-sharp white Cheddar (8 ounces) (see note)

Grate the Cheddar in large shreds on a box grater, as you would grate carrots. For a large amount, you can use the carrot grater blade of your food processor.

If you don't have a panini press, you can make these in a sauté pan with a small skillet on top.

Lay 6 slices of the bread on a cutting board and brush each slice generously with the butter. Turn the slices over and spread each one with 1½ tablespoons of the chutney. Place ½ cup of the Cheddar evenly on each slice and place the remaining 6 slices of bread on top of each sandwich. Brush the tops generously with melted butter.

Heat a panini press (see note) and grill the sandwiches according to the directions for the machine, until the bread is nicely browned on both sides and the cheddar is starting to melt.

Place the sandwiches on a cutting board and cut each one in half diagonally. Serve hot.

baked raclette

All cuisines have their own "comfort food" and often it's based on peasant food. This decadent potato, sausage, and melted cheese dish is a blend of Swiss, French, and Spanish country food and it's simply amazing. Serve it with a big green salad and a crusty baguette, and all your worries will simply melt away.

SERVES 4

1 pound fingerling potatoes
(see note)

Kosher salt and freshly ground
black pepper

Good olive oil

8 ounces chorizo sausages, such
as d'Artagnan, halved lengthwise,
then sliced ½ inch thick diagonally

⅓ cup dry white wine,
such as Chablis

8 ounces cold raclette cheese,
rind removed and thinly sliced
(see note)

6 to 8 sprigs fresh thyme

12 cornichons, sliced in fans
(see note)

Green Salad Vinaigrette
(recipe follows)

Crusty French bread and Dijon
mustard, for serving

Preheat the oven to 450 degrees.

Place the potatoes in a medium pot, cover with water by one inch, add 1 tablespoon salt, and bring to a boil. Simmer for 10 to 15 minutes, until the potatoes are barely tender when tested with a wooden skewer. Drain and cover with a kitchen towel to steam for 5 minutes. Cut in half lengthwise and set aside.

Meanwhile, heat 2 tablespoons olive oil over medium heat in a large (12-inch) sauté pan, add the chorizo, and cook for 8 to 10 minutes, turning often, until browned. Drain all but a tablespoon of the fat from the pan, add the potatoes, and toss to combine with the chorizo and fat. Off the heat, stir in the wine, 1 teaspoon salt, and ½ teaspoon pepper.

Divide the sausage and potatoes among four gratin dishes. Arrange the raclette in one layer over the potatoes and chorizo. Distribute the thyme sprigs on top. Bake for 8 to 10 minutes, until the cheese is hot and bubbly.

Remove the gratins from the oven, place the cornichons on top, and serve hot with the Green Salad Vinaigrette, the bread, and mustard.

---

*Choose similarly sized potatoes
so they all cook in the same
amount of time.*

*To fan the cornichons, slice each
cornichon lengthwise almost to
the stem but not quite and gently
spread the fan open.*

green salad vinaigrette

SERVES 4

1½ tablespoons champagne vinegar

¼ teaspoon Dijon mustard

½ teaspoon minced garlic

1 extra-large egg yolk, at room temperature (see note)

Kosher salt and freshly ground black pepper

¼ cup good olive oil

6 ounces baby arugula or mesclun mix

In a small bowl, whisk together the vinegar, mustard, garlic, egg yolk, ½ teaspoon salt, and ⅛ teaspoon pepper. While whisking, slowly add the olive oil until the vinaigrette is emulsified.

Place the greens in a serving bowl and toss them with enough dressing to moisten. Serve immediately.

If you're worried about eating raw egg, just eliminate it.

Put the vinaigrette in a serving bowl and place the greens on top without tossing. Set aside for up to 30 minutes. Toss and serve.

make ahead: *Wash and spin-dry the greens in a salad spinner and store refrigerated in a plastic bag lined with a paper towel.*

broccoli & kale salad

Jean-Georges Vongerichten is one of the great restaurateurs I've had the privilege to know. His restaurants range from elegant (Jean-Georges) to country (Topping Rose House) to seafood (The Fulton) and I love them all. This salad is inspired by one of his dishes and I could eat it for lunch every day. The Caesar dressing and 6½-minute egg turn a delicious green salad into total comfort food.

SERVES 6

Kosher salt and freshly ground black pepper

8 cups broccoli florets, stems removed (2 bunches)

1 bunch baby kale

Caesar Salad Dressing (recipe follows)

1 cup Toasted Croutons (page 70)

¼ cup freshly squeezed lemon juice (1 to 2 lemons)

¼ cup grated Italian Parmesan cheese

6 extra-large eggs

Bring a large pot of water with 1 tablespoon of salt to a boil and fill a bowl with ice water. Add the broccoli to the boiling water and cook for *exactly* 4 minutes. Remove the broccoli with a slotted spoon and transfer to the bowl of ice water. When cool, drain well and transfer to a large bowl.

Remove and discard any hard ribs from the kale, stack the leaves on top of each other, and thinly julienne them crosswise. Add to the bowl with the broccoli.

Add enough Caesar Dressing to moisten the broccoli and kale and toss well. Add the croutons, lemon juice, and Parmesan. Divide the salad among six dinner plates.

Meanwhile, fill a medium saucepan with water and bring to a boil. With a spoon, carefully lower each of the eggs into the boiling water and lower the heat until the water is at a low simmer. (You don't want the eggs knocking around in the pot or they will crack.) Cook the eggs for 6½ minutes *exactly*, remove them from the saucepan, run them under cool water, and peel (see note). Place one egg on each salad, cut it in half, sprinkle with salt and pepper, and serve immediately.

To peel an egg, rap the ends on a board to crack the shell. Roll the middle of the egg on the board with the heel of your hand to crackle the shell, then peel carefully. Fresh eggs are harder to peel than less fresh ones.

caesar salad dressing

This is my classic Caesar salad dressing. It's important that all the ingredients be at room temperature, particularly the eggs. The dressing will last for a week in the refrigerator.

MAKES 2 CUPS

2 extra-large egg yolks,
at room temperature

2 teaspoons Dijon mustard,
at room temperature

2 teaspoons chopped garlic
(2 cloves)

10 anchovy fillets

½ cup freshly squeezed lemon juice, at room temperature
(2 to 3 lemons)

Kosher salt and freshly ground black pepper

1½ cups good mild olive oil

½ cup freshly grated Italian Parmesan cheese

Place the egg yolks, mustard, garlic, anchovies, lemon juice, 2 teaspoons salt, and ½ teaspoon pepper in the bowl of a food processor fitted with the steel blade and process until smooth. With the food processor running, slowly pour the olive oil through the feed tube (as though you were making mayonnaise) and process until thick. Add the Parmesan and pulse 3 times to combine.

tomato & goat cheese crostata

Crostatas are rustic tarts and they can be either sweet or savory. The flavors in this savory version—roasted tomatoes and cheese—are reminiscent of a grilled cheese & tomato sandwich. The layer of sautéed leeks and goat cheese makes this a very special lunch. Baking it on an upside-down sheet pan ensures that the bottom of the crust browns really nicely.

SERVES 4

FOR THE PASTRY:

1 cup all-purpose flour

Kosher salt

¼ pound (1 stick) very cold unsalted butter, diced

3 tablespoons ice water

FOR THE TART:

4 tablespoons (½ stick) unsalted butter

4 cups chopped leeks, white and light green parts, spun-dried (4 leeks)

1 teaspoon minced fresh thyme leaves

Kosher salt and freshly ground black pepper

1 pound heirloom tomatoes, cored and sliced ⅜ inch thick (see note)

Good olive oil

4 ounces creamy fresh goat cheese, crumbled

1 egg beaten with 1 tablespoon milk, for egg wash

Chopped fresh basil leaves and chives

For the pastry, place the flour and ½ teaspoon salt in the bowl of a food processor fitted with the steel blade and pulse to combine. Add the diced butter and toss carefully with your fingers to coat each piece of butter with flour. Pulse 12 to 15 times, until the butter is the size of peas. While pulsing, add the ice water all at once through the feed tube. Pulse to combine, stopping just before the dough forms a ball. Turn the dough out onto a well-floured board and form it into a disk. Wrap in plastic and refrigerate for one hour.

Meanwhile, preheat the oven to 450 degrees. Heat the 4 tablespoons butter in a large (12-inch) sauté pan over medium to medium-high heat. Add the leeks, thyme, 1 teaspoon salt, and ½ teaspoon pepper and sauté for 8 minutes, until the leeks are tender and starting to brown. Set aside. Place the tomatoes on a plate, sprinkle them with salt and pepper, and drizzle lightly with olive oil. Set aside.

On a floured board, roll the dough to an 11-inch circle, then place it on a sheet of parchment paper. Turn a sheet pan upside down and transfer the paper to the inverted pan. Spread the leeks on the pastry, leaving a 1½-inch border. Crumble the goat cheese evenly on top. Arrange the tomatoes over the goat cheese, overlapping the slices because they will shrink. Turn the edges of the pastry up and over the tomatoes, crimping so they lie flat. Brush the pastry with the egg wash. Bake for 25 to 30 minutes, until the pastry is nicely browned. Allow to cool on the pan for 5 minutes, sprinkle lightly with the fresh herbs and salt, cut in wedges, and serve warm.

Cut the tomatoes crosswise with a serrated knife. Use only the beautiful center slices.

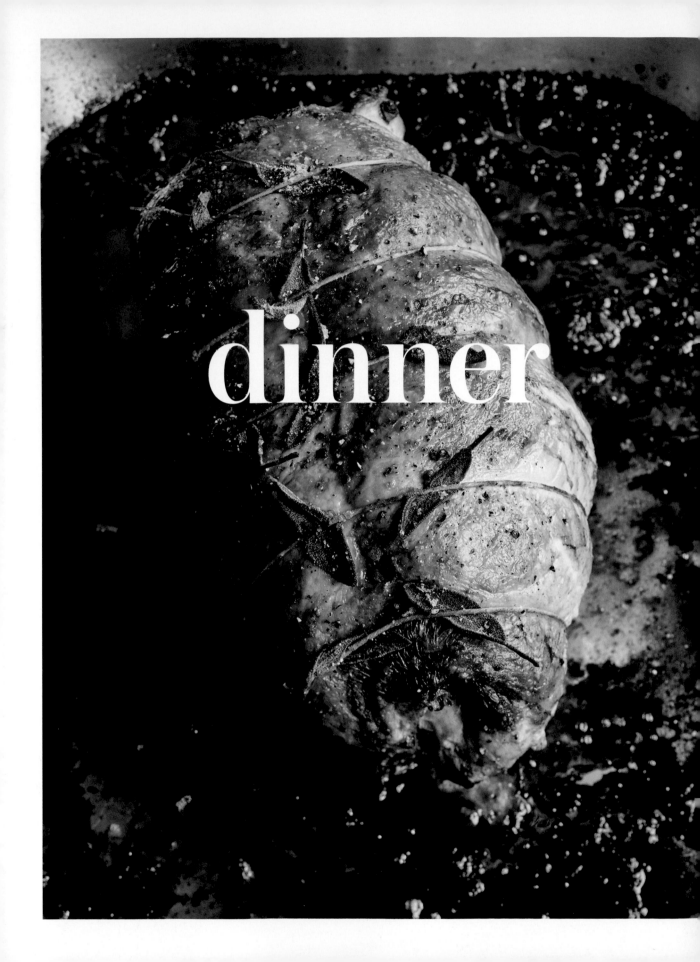

dinner

ultimate beef stew

———

tuscan turkey roulade

———

skillet-roasted chicken & potatoes

———

crispy chicken with lemon orzo

———

cheesy chicken enchiladas

———

smashed hamburgers with caramelized onions

———

steak fajitas

———

roasted sausages, peppers & onions

———

seared salmon with spicy red pepper aioli

———

baked cod with garlic & herb ritz crumbs

CONTINUES »

shellfish & chorizo stew

—

brussels sprouts pizza carbonara

—

shrimp & linguine fra diavolo

—

fresh crab & pea risotto

—

baked rigatoni with lamb ragù

—

spring green spaghetti carbonara

—

truffled mac & cheese

—

spaghetti squash arrabbiata

—

staying engaged

Jeffrey and I have a friend, Jack Rowe, who we adore. He's a physician who specializes in geriatrics, or the care of older people. He told us a story that has always stayed with me. Jack asks his Columbia medical school class to interview an older patient to determine their life expectancy. He instructs the students to not bother asking about their diagnoses, diet, or exercise, which are the first things you'd think would be relevant, right? Instead, he wants the students to focus on two things: first, how many people has the person interacted with over the past week? Do they have friends they see, family that drops in on them? Second, do they have hobbies and interests they're engaged in? Are they involved with any charities? Do they travel, garden, have pets, or play cards regularly with friends? As Jack knew a long time ago (and as was confirmed recently by a large research study), loneliness is an epidemic in this country and may be a more important predictor of longevity than diet and exercise.

What's all this got to do with cooking? Well, it turns out dinner parties aren't just a fun way to pass the time, they're also good for your health! In an era of 24/7 social media that's meant to connect all of us, it turns out that we're lonelier and more in need of meaningful relationships than ever before. Entertaining and cooking is a powerful way not just to nourish people but also to enrich your life and stay connected to the people you love. No matter how old we are, we all benefit from putting down our cell phones and enjoying one another's company face-to-face.

I hope this book inspires you to take the time to cook for the people in your life. Whether you're a beginner or an experienced cook, these recipes will help you feel confident that you can cook wonderful food for your family and friends and that will bring everyone to your table. And if you end up being happier—and healthier!—because of it, so much the better!

ultimate beef stew

Beef stew is the quintessential winter comfort food but I usually find it boring. I kept the classic vegetables like potatoes, carrots, and peas but ramped up the flavor of the stew by using boneless short ribs instead of the usual chuck, plus lots of full-bodied red wine and Cognac for the sauce. This is definitely the most satisfying beef stew I've ever made!

SERVES 6 TO 8

3 tablespoons good olive oil

4 ounces small-diced pancetta (see note)

3 pounds boneless short ribs, cut in 1½-inch chunks (4½ pounds on the bone)

Kosher salt and freshly ground black pepper

¼ cup Cognac or brandy

1 cup hearty red wine, such as a Côtes du Rhône or Chianti, divided

2 cups chopped yellow onions (2 onions)

2 cups chopped fennel, trimmed and cored (1 large bulb)

2 tablespoons minced garlic (6 cloves)

1 (14.5-ounce) can diced tomatoes, including the juices

2 tablespoons tomato paste

2 cups beef broth, such as College Inn

1 pound carrots, scrubbed and cut ½ inch thick diagonally

1 pound Yukon Gold potatoes, scrubbed, 1-inch diced

10 ounces frozen peas

Preheat the oven to 300 degrees.

Heat the oil in a large (11 to 12-inch) Dutch oven over medium heat. Add the pancetta and cook for 4 to 5 minutes, until browned. With a slotted spoon, transfer the pancetta to a plate lined with a paper towel and set aside.

Meanwhile, season the short ribs all over with 2 teaspoons salt and 1 teaspoon pepper. Brown half the meat in the Dutch oven over medium heat, turning occasionally, for 5 to 7 minutes, until browned on all sides. Transfer the meat to a bowl and brown the second batch. (Don't cook them all in one batch or they won't brown!) Transfer the second batch to the bowl and set aside.

Off the heat, add the Cognac and ⅓ cup of the wine to the pot, scraping up any browned bits, then simmer over medium heat for one minute. Add the onions and fennel and sauté, stirring occasionally, for 7 to 8 minutes, until the vegetables are tender. Add the garlic and cook for one minute.

Stir the tomatoes and tomato paste into the vegetables. Add the remaining ⅔ cup of wine, the beef broth, the seared meat (and juices), 2 teaspoons salt, and 1 teaspoon pepper. Bring to a simmer, cover, and bake for 1¼ hours, checking occasionally to be sure the liquid is simmering.

Degrease the stew, if necessary. Stir in the carrots and potatoes, cover, and bake for one hour longer, until the vegetables and meat are very tender when tested with a fork. Just before serving, stir in the peas and pancetta, taste for seasonings, and serve hot in large, shallow bowls.

Citterio makes a 4-ounce package of perfectly diced pancetta.

make ahead: *Reheat over medium-low heat, adding beef broth and a splash of red wine.*

tuscan turkey roulade

Why do we eat turkey only on Thanksgiving?? If it's prepared properly, turkey can be delicious and easy for any dinner party. This turkey roulade is actually better if you assemble it in advance because the flavors—prosciutto, fennel seeds, garlic, fresh sage, and rosemary—all permeate the turkey. This is classic comfort food with the volume turned up.

SERVES 8 TO 10

Good olive oil

1½ cups chopped yellow onion (1 large)

¾ teaspoon whole fennel seeds

2 tablespoons minced garlic (6 cloves)

1 tablespoon chopped fresh sage leaves, plus 4 whole sage leaves

1 tablespoon minced fresh rosemary leaves

1 whole butterflied boneless turkey breast with the skin on (5 to 6 pounds) (see note)

Kosher salt and freshly ground black pepper

4 tablespoons (½ stick) cold unsalted butter

4 ounces thinly sliced Italian prosciutto

1 cup dry white wine, such as Chablis

A whole turkey breast refers to the two breasts of one turkey, with the skin connecting them.

Grate the butter on a box grater, as you would grate carrots.

Preheat the oven to 350 degrees.

Heat 2 tablespoons olive oil in a medium (10 to 11-inch) sauté pan over medium heat. Add the onion and fennel seeds and cook for 6 to 8 minutes, tossing occasionally, until the onion is tender. Add the garlic and cook for one minute. Off the heat, add the chopped sage and the rosemary and set aside to cool.

Meanwhile, open the turkey breast on a cutting board, skin side down. Sprinkle the meat with 4 teaspoons salt and 1½ teaspoons pepper. When the onion mixture is cool, spread it evenly on the meat. Grate the butter (see note) and sprinkle it on top. Arrange the prosciutto on top to totally cover the meat and filling.

Starting at one long end of the turkey breast, roll the meat up jelly-roll style to make a compact cylindrical roulade, ending with the seam side down. Tie the roulade tightly with kitchen twine at 2 to 2½-inch intervals to ensure that it will roast evenly. Slip the whole sage leaves under the twine down the center of the roulade.

Place the roulade, seam side down, in a roasting pan and pat the skin dry with paper towels. Brush the skin with 2 tablespoons olive oil and sprinkle with 1 teaspoon salt and ½ teaspoon pepper. Pour the wine and 1 cup of water in the roasting pan (not over the turkey). Roast for 1½ to 1¾ hours, until the skin is golden brown and the internal temperature is 150 degrees. Remove from the oven, cover with foil, and allow to rest for 15 minutes. Remove the string, slice crosswise in ½-inch-thick slices, and serve warm with the pan juices.

skillet-roasted chicken & potatoes

*Any roast chicken is comfort food to me, but roast it in a cast-iron skillet with garlic,
potatoes, mustard, and white wine and I'm in! If you marinate the chicken in the morning,
it takes no time to cook when you get home from work and the skillet can go from the oven
directly to the table! This is a great weeknight dinner.*

SERVES 4

4 large bone-in, skin-on chicken
thighs (2½ to 3 pounds total)

Kosher salt and freshly ground
black pepper

2½ cups buttermilk, shaken

Good olive oil

2 tablespoons Dijon mustard

1 tablespoon dry white wine,
such as Chablis

1½ teaspoons fresh thyme leaves

⅛ teaspoon sweet Hungarian
paprika

1 pound medium Yukon Gold
potatoes, unpeeled, sliced
¼ inch thick

1 tablespoon minced garlic
(3 cloves)

2 tablespoons minced fresh
parsley

1 tablespoon chopped fresh chives

At least 4 hours (but not more than 12 hours) before
you plan to serve, sprinkle the chicken all over with
1 teaspoon salt and ½ teaspoon pepper. Place in a
1-gallon sealable plastic bag and pour in the buttermilk.
Seal the bag and massage it lightly to be sure the chicken
is coated with the buttermilk. Place in the refrigerator to
marinate.

Preheat the oven to 350 degrees. Pour 2 tablespoons olive
oil in an unheated 12-inch cast-iron skillet and tilt the
pan so the oil covers the bottom. Lift the thighs out of
the buttermilk, letting any excess buttermilk drip off,
and place them in the skillet, skin side up, in one layer.
Discard the marinade. In a small bowl, combine the
mustard and wine and brush it on the top of the chicken.
Sprinkle with the thyme, paprika, 1 teaspoon salt, and
½ teaspoon pepper. Place the skillet in the oven and
roast the chicken for 30 minutes.

Using tongs, transfer the chicken to a plate and put
the potatoes, garlic, 1 teaspoon salt, and ½ teaspoon
pepper into the skillet. Toss to coat with the pan juices
then spread the potatoes out. Return the chicken to
the skillet, placing it on the potatoes. Roast 30 minutes
longer, until the chicken registers 155 degrees on an
instant-read thermometer. Transfer just the chicken
to a plate and cover loosely with aluminum foil to
keep warm. Return the skillet to the oven, raise the
temperature to 425 degrees, and roast the potatoes for
15 minutes, until they're tender and starting to brown.
Return the chicken to the pan and sprinkle with the
parsley, chives, and extra salt. Serve hot from the skillet.

crispy chicken with lemon orzo

For this chicken dish, I was inspired by the classic Italian method of cooking chicken breasts "al burro," or in butter. Then I gave it a Greek twist by serving it with orzo, feta, and dill. High-temperature cooking seals in the juices and makes the skin really crispy.

SERVES 4

⅔ cup all-purpose flour

Kosher salt and freshly ground black pepper

4 boneless chicken breasts, skin-on (about 8 ounces each)

¼ cup canola oil

9 tablespoons good European-style unsalted butter, such as Plugrá, divided

2 tablespoons minced fresh parsley

Lemon Orzo with Feta (recipe follows)

1 lemon, cut into 8 wedges

European butters have lower water content and help the chicken sear better than domestic butters.

Preheat the oven to 450 degrees.

Combine the flour, 2 teaspoons salt, and 1 teaspoon pepper in a shallow bowl. Remove the tenders on the underside of the chicken breasts and save for another use. (This makes the chicken breasts an even thickness so they cook evenly.) Heat the canola oil and 4 tablespoons of the butter together in a large (12-inch) cast-iron skillet over medium heat until the butter has melted and begins to sizzle.

Dredge the chicken in the flour mixture and shake off any excess. Place the chicken, skin side down, in the skillet and cook over medium heat *without moving* for 12 minutes. With the chicken still skin side down, place the skillet in the oven and roast for 10 minutes.

Return the skillet to the stovetop over medium heat (careful; the handle will be hot!). Turn the chicken skin side up, add the remaining 5 tablespoons of butter, and continue cooking for 3 to 5 minutes, until the butter is a nutty brown color and the chicken breasts are just cooked through (an instant-read thermometer will register 130 to 140 degrees). Off the heat, sprinkle on the parsley.

Divide the Lemon Orzo with Feta among four dinner plates. Transfer the chicken to a cutting board and slice each breast crosswise in thick slices. Arrange one breast on each plate with the orzo. Spoon a few tablespoons of the brown butter over each chicken breast, squeeze on some lemon, and sprinkle with salt. Serve hot with a fresh wedge of lemon on each plate.

lemon orzo with feta

SERVES 4

Kosher salt and freshly ground black pepper

1 cup orzo

2 teaspoons grated lemon zest

2 tablespoons freshly squeezed lemon juice

2 tablespoons good olive oil

1 tablespoon minced fresh dill

1 cup small-diced feta, preferably Greek (4 ounces)

In a large saucepan, bring 2 quarts of water to a boil. Add 2 teaspoons salt and the orzo. Return the water to a boil and simmer uncovered for 9 to 11 minutes, until the orzo is al dente. Drain.

Transfer the orzo to a bowl and stir in the lemon zest, lemon juice, olive oil, dill, 2 teaspoons salt, and 1 teaspoon pepper. Fold in the feta and serve hot.

cheesy chicken enchiladas

So much Mexican food is comfort food, especially the warm, cheesy, spicy dishes with wonderful sauces like enchiladas. These are filled with roasted chicken, fire-roasted tomatoes, poblano pepper, black beans, and chipotle powder. Then I bake them with homemade enchilada sauce, goat cheese, and Cheddar. Of course, you can also use leftover roast chicken!

SERVES 4 TO 6

2 pounds chicken breasts, bone-in, skin-on (3 split)

Good olive oil

Kosher salt and freshly ground black pepper

2 tablespoons canola oil

2 tablespoons all-purpose flour

1 tablespoon chili powder

1 tablespoon ground chipotle powder

1 teaspoon ground cumin

2 cups good chicken stock, preferably homemade (page 64)

1 (14.5-ounce) can fire-roasted diced tomatoes

1½ cups crushed tomatoes, such as San Marzano

1 teaspoon dried oregano, crushed in your hands

1½ cups chopped yellow onion (1 large)

½ cup seeded and small-diced poblano pepper

1 (15.5-ounce) can black beans, rinsed and drained

¼ cup minced fresh parsley or cilantro, plus extra for garnish

7 (8-inch) flour tortillas

7 ounces creamy goat cheese, such as Montrachet

2 cups freshly grated extra-sharp white Cheddar (6 ounces)

Sour cream, for serving

2 ripe Hass avocados, pitted, peeled, and sliced, for serving

make ahead: *Assemble the dish completely and refrigerate for up to a day. Bake straight from the refrigerator at 350 degrees for 40 to 45 minutes, until hot and bubbly.*

Preheat the oven to 350 degrees.

Place the chicken on a sheet pan skin side up, rub with olive oil, and sprinkle with salt and black pepper. Roast for 30 to 40 minutes, until a thermometer registers 140 degrees. Cover with aluminum foil and set aside for 15 minutes, until cool enough to handle. Discard the skin and bones and shred the chicken in bite-size pieces.

Meanwhile, heat the canola oil in a large saucepan over medium heat and whisk in the flour. Cook, whisking constantly, for one minute, then whisk in the chili powder, chipotle powder, and cumin. Add the stock, bring to a boil, lower the heat, and simmer for a few minutes until slightly thickened. Stir in the fire-roasted tomatoes, crushed tomatoes, oregano, and 1 tablespoon salt, bring to a boil, then lower the heat and simmer for 20 minutes, stirring occasionally.

Meanwhile, make the filling. Heat 2 tablespoons olive oil over medium-high heat in a medium (10 to 11-inch) sauté pan, add the onion and poblano pepper, and sauté for 5 to 7 minutes, until tender. Off the heat, stir in the shredded chicken, black beans, parsley, 1½ teaspoons salt, and ½ teaspoon black pepper and set aside.

To assemble, spread 1 cup of the sauce in a 9 × 13-inch baking dish. Lay one tortilla on a board and spread it with 3 tablespoons of the sauce. Spoon ¾ cup of the filling down the middle of the tortilla. Crumble 1 ounce of goat cheese on the filling. Roll the tortilla up tightly and place it seam side down in the baking dish. Repeat to make 6 more enchiladas and place them snugly side by side in the dish. Spread the remaining sauce on top and sprinkle with the Cheddar.

Bake for 30 to 35 minutes, until the cheese is melted and the sauce is bubbly. Sprinkle with parsley and serve hot with sour cream and avocados.

smashed hamburgers with carmelized onions

Could there possibly be a new way to make hamburgers that I didn't know about?? As it turns out, there is! You form the burgers and freeze them for fifteen minutes, then sear them in a hot cast-iron skillet (smashing them lightly with a metal spatula) so the outsides get browned and crusty while the insides are still rare. I love the caramelized onions and melted Gruyère on top.

MAKES 4 HAMBURGERS

Canola or grapeseed oil

4 cups (¼-inch) sliced red onions (2 medium)

1 teaspoon sugar

1 tablespoon good red wine vinegar

1½ teaspoons dry mustard powder, such as Colman's

Kosher salt and freshly ground black pepper

1¼ pounds ground beef with 20% fat

1¼ cups grated Gruyère cheese (4 ounces)

4 sandwich potato rolls, such as Martin's

Ketchup, for serving

Heat 2 tablespoons oil in a large (12-inch) sauté pan over medium heat, add the onions, and cook for 8 to 10 minutes, stirring occasionally, until the onions are tender and starting to brown. Add the sugar, reduce the heat to low, and cook for 10 to 15 minutes, stirring occasionally, until the onions are browned and caramelized. Add the vinegar and cook for 30 seconds to deglaze the pan.

Meanwhile, combine the dry mustard, 1½ teaspoons salt, and ½ teaspoon pepper in a small bowl. Place the ground beef in a medium bowl and sprinkle on the mustard mixture. With your fingers, lightly work the mustard into the beef and shape into four 1-inch-thick patties. Place them on a plate and freeze for *exactly* 15 minutes.

Heat a large (12-inch) cast-iron skillet over medium-high heat and add 1½ tablespoons oil. From the freezer, place the burgers directly in the hot skillet. With a large metal spatula, firmly press each burger into the pan. Cook the burgers for 2½ to 3 minutes, without moving them, so the bottoms get browned and crusty. Flip the burgers, then spoon on the onions and sprinkle the Gruyère on top. Place a lid on the skillet and cook the burgers for 1½ to 2 minutes, until the cheese is melted and the burgers are medium-rare inside. Place one burger on each roll and serve hot with ketchup on the side.

steak fajitas

There used to be a Tex-Mex restaurant in East Hampton called Little Rock Rodeo and we loved their fajitas. This is a remembered flavor for me; I tried to duplicate those fajitas with seared steak, sweet peppers, hot peppers, onions, and lots of good cheese on top.

MAKES 6 FAJITAS / SERVES 3

1 (1½-inch-thick) New York strip steak (about ¾ pound)

Kosher salt

Good olive oil

1 teaspoon whole cumin seeds

1 Holland yellow bell pepper, cored, seeded, and cut in ¼-inch-wide strips

1 Holland orange bell pepper, cored, seeded, and cut in ¼-inch-wide strips

1 poblano pepper, seeded and cut in ¼-inch-wide strips

1 large jalapeño pepper, seeded and cut in very thin strips

1 medium red onion, halved and thinly sliced in half-rounds

1 tablespoon minced garlic (3 cloves)

6 (8-inch) flour tortillas

6 ounces grated Monterey Jack cheese

6 ounces grated Manchego cheese (not aged)

Sliced scallions, white and green parts, for serving

Preheat the oven to 400 degrees.

Heat a large (12-inch) cast-iron skillet over medium-high heat for 3 minutes. Pat the steak dry with paper towels and sprinkle it generously on both sides with salt. Sear the steak in the hot dry skillet for 2 minutes on each side, then place the skillet in the oven and roast the steak for 4 minutes. Remove from the oven, place the steak on a plate, cover with aluminum foil, and allow to rest for 12 minutes. Lower the oven to 350 degrees.

Pour 2 tablespoons olive oil into the same skillet and heat over medium-high heat. Add the cumin seeds and sauté for 1 to 1½ minutes, until fragrant. Add all four peppers and the red onion and sauté for 10 minutes, stirring occasionally, until the vegetables are tender and beginning to blister and brown. About halfway through, stir in the garlic and 2 teaspoons salt. Remove from the heat and slice the steak crosswise ¼ inch thick. Stir the steak and the juices into the vegetables.

Meanwhile, wrap the tortillas in aluminum foil and heat them in the oven for 10 to 15 minutes. Combine the two cheeses in a bowl.

Lay one tortilla on a plate and sprinkle on some of the cheese, leaving a border. Spoon some steak and vegetables on top, sprinkle with scallions, and roll up tight. Repeat for the remaining five tortillas and serve hot.

You can also serve this family-style: place the skillet on the table with a plate of the warm tortillas and a bowl with the cheeses, and let everyone assemble their own fajitas.

Of course, you can double this recipe but be sure to use a bigger pan so the ingredients sauté instead of steaming.

roasted sausages, peppers & onions

Is there anything more satisfying than an old-fashioned Italian sausage and pepper hero?
Yes! It's sausages and peppers served on a big puddle of Fresh Corn Polenta (page 172).
This is a true stick-to-your-ribs dinner updated to roast in the oven so cleanup is a snap.
I love the mixture of spicy and sweet sausages with the poblano peppers that add a little
heat and a smoky note.

SERVES 6

2 large yellow onions, cut in
½-inch-wide wedges through
the core

2 large Holland red bell peppers,
cored, seeded, and cut in
½-inch strips

2 large Holland orange bell
peppers, cored, seeded, and
cut in ½-inch strips

2 large poblano peppers, seeded
and cut in ¼-inch strips

1 medium fennel bulb, halved,
cored, and sliced crosswise
¼ inch thick

2 tablespoons minced garlic
(6 cloves)

1 teaspoon dried oregano, crushed
in your hands

Kosher salt and freshly ground
black pepper

Good olive oil

1 pound sweet Italian sausage,
cut into links

1 pound hot Italian sausage,
cut into links

1 pint red cherry tomatoes

⅓ cup dry white wine, such as
Pinot Grigio

½ cup julienned fresh basil leaves

Freshly grated Italian Parmesan
cheese, for serving

Preheat the oven to 400 degrees. Arrange two racks
evenly spaced in the oven.

Put the onions, Holland peppers, poblano peppers, fennel,
garlic, oregano, 1 tablespoon salt, and 1½ teaspoons
black pepper in a large (14 × 18-inch), shallow roasting
pan. Add ¼ cup olive oil and toss well. (Don't crowd
everything in a smaller pan; the vegetables won't brown.)
Separately, on a sheet pan, toss the sausages with
2 tablespoons olive oil and spread them out in one layer.
Place both pans in the oven for 20 minutes.

Toss the vegetables and transfer the sausages to the
roasting pan. Add the tomatoes. Pour in the wine and
roast for another 25 to 30 minutes, turning the sausages
to brown evenly. Off the heat, sprinkle on the basil, toss
well, taste for seasonings, and serve hot with grated
Parmesan on the side.

*Poblano peppers
are chili peppers
from Mexico.*

seared salmon with spicy red pepper aioli

Steakhouses cook steaks by searing the outside over high heat on top of the stove and then finishing them in the oven. The same method works for salmon—the key is to get your cast-iron skillet very hot, add the fillets, and don't move them for two minutes before flipping them and putting the pan in the oven. The salmon ends up crusty outside and moist inside. My spicy aioli makes it even better!

SERVES 4

2 teaspoons minced garlic
(2 cloves)

1 tablespoon (canned) chopped chipotle pepper in adobo sauce

1 tablespoon freshly squeezed lime juice

¼ cup jarred roasted red peppers, seeded and chopped

1 cup good mayonnaise, such as Hellmann's

Kosher salt and freshly ground black pepper

4 (6-ounce) boneless, skinless, center-cut salmon fillets

Good olive oil

1 lime, quartered, for serving

make ahead: *The aioli will keep in the refrigerator for at least 5 days.*

Preheat the oven to 400 degrees.

For the aioli, chop the garlic and chipotle pepper together on a cutting board to make a coarse paste. Place the paste in a food processor, add the lime juice and roasted red peppers, and purée. Add the mayonnaise, ¼ teaspoon salt, and ¼ teaspoon black pepper and process until smooth. Set aside.

For the salmon, place a large (12-inch), dry cast-iron skillet over high heat for 5 minutes. Place the salmon fillets on a board, pat dry with paper towels, and rub all over with olive oil. With the fillets *rounded side up*, sprinkle them with 1½ teaspoons salt and ¾ teaspoon black pepper.

Place the salmon in the skillet *rounded side down* and cook over medium-high heat for exactly 2 minutes without moving! Using a large metal spatula, turn the fillets rounded side up and place the skillet in the oven. Roast for 3 to 4 minutes, until the centers are rare. Cover the pan loosely with aluminum foil and allow the salmon to rest for 3 to 4 minutes for medium-rare or 5 minutes for medium. Serve the salmon hot with the aioli and a wedge of lime for squeezing.

baked cod with garlic & herb ritz crumbs

The late cookbook writer Lee Bailey used to say that he never served fish at parties because you'd eat it fast and then be out the door in five minutes! This is a fish dish that you'll want to sit and savor. The tender white cod fillets are cooked in white wine and fresh lemon juice with a crunchy topping of old-fashioned Ritz crackers, panko crumbs, and lemon zest. Very retro but so new and delicious!

SERVES 4

Good olive oil

4 center-cut boneless, skinless cod fillets (6 to 8 ounces each)

Kosher salt and freshly ground black pepper

½ cup Ritz cracker crumbs (15 crackers) (see note)

⅓ cup panko (Japanese bread flakes)

2 tablespoons minced fresh parsley

2 teaspoons minced garlic (2 cloves)

1 teaspoon grated lemon zest

3 tablespoons unsalted butter, melted

¼ cup dry white wine, such as Pinot Grigio

2 tablespoons freshly squeezed lemon juice

Lemon wedges, for serving

Preheat the oven to 400 degrees.

Pour 2 tablespoons olive oil in a 9 × 9-inch ceramic baking dish (it should be just big enough to hold the fish) and tilt the dish to coat the bottom with oil. Place the fish fillets in the dish and turn to coat both sides with the oil. Sprinkle the fish with 1½ teaspoons salt and ½ teaspoon pepper and bake for 10 minutes.

Meanwhile, combine the cracker crumbs, panko, parsley, garlic, lemon zest, and 1 teaspoon salt in a small bowl. Add the melted butter and stir until evenly moistened. Set aside.

Remove the fish from the oven and pour the wine and lemon juice directly on the fillets. Pat the crumb mixture evenly onto the fillets, pressing gently to help them adhere. (Don't worry if some crumbs get into the sauce!)

Return the pan to the oven for 12 minutes, until the fillets are just cooked through in the center, depending on the thickness of the fish. Sprinkle with salt and serve hot with the pan juices and lemon wedges.

To make the crumbs, crush the Ritz crackers into the bowl of a food processor fitted with the steel blade and process until finely ground.

shellfish & chorizo stew

I love dinners where you cook everything in one big pot. All the flavors blend together and cleanup is a snap. This shellfish stew has scallops, clams, and mussels, along with spicy chorizo, which flavors everything else. It's old-fashioned but with fresh flavors and so satisfying.

SERVES 4

¾ pound baby potatoes, unpeeled, halved if larger than 1 inch

Kosher salt and freshly ground black pepper

2 tablespoons unsalted butter

1 tablespoon good olive oil

2 cups chopped yellow onion (2 onions)

1 tablespoon minced garlic (3 cloves)

4 ounces Spanish-style chorizo, halved lengthwise and sliced ½ inch thick (see note)

1 tablespoon minced fresh tarragon leaves

1½ cups dry white wine, such as Chablis or Pinot Grigio

1½ cups heavy cream

¾ pound fresh sea scallops, side muscles removed, halved

2 pounds fresh littleneck clams, scrubbed

1 pound fresh mussels, scrubbed and debearded (see note)

Minced fresh parsley and crusty baguette, for serving

Place the potatoes and 1 tablespoon salt in a medium saucepan and cover generously with water. Bring to a boil, lower the heat, and simmer for 8 to 10 minutes, until barely tender. Drain and set aside.

Meanwhile, heat the butter and olive oil in a large (11 to 12-inch) stockpot or Dutch oven, such as Le Creuset, over medium-low heat. Add the onions and sauté for 7 to 10 minutes, until translucent but not browned. Add the garlic and chorizo and cook for 5 to 7 minutes, stirring occasionally, until the chorizo has started to crisp. Stir in the tarragon, cook for one minute, then add the wine and simmer for 5 to 7 minutes, until reduced by half.

Add the cream, 2 teaspoons salt, 1 teaspoon pepper, and the potatoes. Bring to a boil, lower the heat, and simmer for 4 to 5 minutes, until the stock is slightly thickened. Stir in the scallops and place the clams and mussels on top. Bring to a boil, lower the heat, and simmer covered for 8 to 10 minutes, until all the shells are opened. (Discard any that don't open.) Taste for seasonings, ladle into large shallow bowls, sprinkle with parsley, and serve hot with chunks of crusty baguette.

There are many types of chorizo; I prefer D'Artagnan chorizo, which is more tender, but you can also use a drier Spanish chorizo. I cut it 45 degrees diagonally to make large pieces.

Almost all mussels today are farmed so they don't have beards and aren't gritty. If yours are wild, pull off the little beards sticking out of the shells and soak the mussels in a large bowl of water with a few tablespoons of flour for 30 minutes to get the mussels to disgorge any grit.

brussels sprouts pizza carbonara

Danny Meyer has many fabulous restaurants, including Marta, in New York City, which is like a Roman trattoria. I'm glad I don't live next door because if I did, I would eat pizza every night! Their pizza with shaved Brussels sprouts inspired these individual pizzas with salty pancetta, creamy ricotta, and crispy sprouts.

MAKES FOUR 9-INCH
INDIVIDUAL PIZZAS

FOR THE BÉCHAMEL:

1½ cups whole milk

2 tablespoons unsalted butter

2 tablespoons all-purpose flour

1 cup whole milk ricotta
(9 ounces)

2 extra-large egg yolks

Kosher salt and freshly ground
black pepper

Good olive oil

8 ounces pancetta, ⅛-inch diced

TO ASSEMBLE THE PIZZAS:

4 (8-ounce) balls store-bought
pizza dough

½ cup freshly grated Italian
Parmesan cheese

½ cup freshly grated Italian
Pecorino cheese

12 ounces Brussels sprouts,
trimmed and thinly sliced
(see note)

To slice the Brussels sprouts, trim them and process through the feed tube of a food processor fitted with the slicing disk.

Preheat the oven to 475 degrees. Arrange two racks evenly spaced in the oven.

For the béchamel, pour the milk into a small saucepan and bring to a simmer over medium heat. Meanwhile, melt the butter in a medium saucepan over medium-low heat. Whisk the flour into the butter and cook for 2 minutes, whisking almost constantly. Whisk in the hot milk, switch to a wooden spoon, and simmer, stirring constantly, for 2 to 5 minutes, until thick enough to leave a trail when you run your finger down the back of the spoon. Cook for one more minute. Off the heat, stir in the ricotta, egg yolks, 1 teaspoon salt, and ½ teaspoon pepper; set aside.

Heat 1 tablespoon olive oil in a medium (10 to 11-inch) sauté pan, add the pancetta, and cook over medium heat for 4 minutes, stirring occasionally, until half-cooked. Transfer the pancetta to a plate lined with paper towels and set aside.

Flip over two sheet pans and put 12 × 18-inch pieces of parchment paper on each pan. Roll and stretch 2 of the pizza doughs into a 9 or 10-inch circle (they don't want to be perfect!) on the parchment papers. Leaving a 1-inch border, spread ½ cup of the béchamel on each pizza and sprinkle with 2 tablespoons of the Parmesan, 2 tablespoons of the Pecorino, and a quarter of the pancetta. In a medium bowl, toss the Brussels sprouts with 3 tablespoons olive oil. Sprinkle the two pizzas evenly with half of the Brussels sprouts. Bake for 15 to 20 minutes, until the crust is nicely browned, including the bottom. Cut each pizza in 6 wedges with a large chef's knife and serve hot. Repeat for the remaining two pizzas.

shrimp & linguine fra diavolo

Pasta with shrimp and a spicy red sauce definitely qualifies as comfort food. This dish is packed with flavors—lots of caramelized red onions, garlic, and spicy arrabbiata sauce. You can certainly make your own sauce but sometimes I make it easy by using jarred Rao's sauce, which is really good!

SERVES 6

3 tablespoons unsalted butter, divided

⅓ cup panko (Japanese bread flakes)

8 tablespoons chopped fresh parsley, divided

Kosher salt and freshly ground black pepper

1¼ pounds large (16 to 20-count) shrimp, peeled and deveined

2 tablespoons good olive oil

2 cups thinly sliced red onion (1 large) (see note)

2 tablespoons minced garlic (6 cloves)

¼ teaspoon crushed red pepper flakes

⅔ cup dry white wine, such as Pinot Grigio

Arrabbiata Sauce, homemade (page 142) or 1 (24-ounce) jar Rao's

1 pound linguine, such as De Cecco

Cut the onion in half through the stem, peel it, leaving the root intact, and slice it thinly crosswise to make half-rounds.

Melt 1 tablespoon of the butter in a medium (10 to 11-inch) sauté pan over medium heat. Add the panko and cook for 2 minutes, stirring occasionally, until nicely browned. Transfer to a small bowl and stir in 2 tablespoons of the parsley, ¼ teaspoon salt, and a pinch of black pepper and set aside.

Place the shrimp on a plate and pat them dry with paper towels. Sprinkle with ½ teaspoon salt and ¼ teaspoon black pepper. Heat the remaining 2 tablespoons of butter and the olive oil in a large (11 to 12-inch) pot over medium heat. Add the onion and sauté for 4 minutes, until it begins to soften. Add the garlic and red pepper flakes and sauté for one minute. Add the shrimp in one layer and sauté for one minute on each side, until they start to turn pink but are not cooked through. Add the wine and simmer for 2 to 3 minutes to reduce the liquid. Stir in the arrabbiata sauce and heat until it simmers. Stir in the remaining 6 tablespoons of parsley with 1 teaspoon salt and ½ teaspoon black pepper and turn off the heat.

Meanwhile, fill a very large pot with water, add 2 tablespoons salt, and bring to a boil. Add the linguine and cook according to the directions on the package for al dente. Reserve a cup of the pasta water, drain the pasta, and add it to the sauce. Toss the pasta, sauce, and shrimp together with tongs or big spoons and allow it to simmer for one minute for the pasta to absorb the sauce, adding enough pasta water to make a nice sauce and coat the pasta. Transfer to a large, shallow serving bowl, sprinkle with the toasted panko, and serve hot.

fresh crab & pea risotto

The key to perfect risotto is getting the heat just right. If you simmer it on too low heat, the rice gets gummy; if you cook it on too high heat, the rice never fully cooks in the middle. But if you simmer it over medium-low heat for 25 to 30 minutes, you'll have perfect risotto every time. White wine, shallots, fresh crabmeat, peas, chives, spicy saffron, smoky poblano pepper, and a hint of lemon at the end make this risotto particularly good.

SERVES 4 TO 6

6 to 8 cups good seafood stock (see note)

2 tablespoons unsalted butter

2 tablespoons good olive oil

½ cup small-diced shallots (2 large)

½ cup chopped fennel, cored

½ cup seeded and small-diced poblano pepper

2 teaspoons minced garlic (2 cloves)

1 teaspoon fresh thyme leaves

½ teaspoon saffron threads

½ teaspoon crushed red pepper flakes

1½ cups Italian Arborio rice (10 ounces)

1 cup dry white wine, such as Pinot Grigio

½ cup crème fraîche

Kosher salt and freshly ground black pepper

16 ounces very good fresh lump crabmeat, picked through for shells

1 cup frozen peas, defrosted

Minced fresh chives and freshly grated lemon zest, for serving

Heat the stock in a medium saucepan and keep it simmering over low heat.

In a medium (10 to 11-inch) pot or Dutch oven, such as Le Creuset, heat the butter and olive oil over medium heat. Add the shallots, fennel, and poblano pepper and cook for 5 minutes, stirring occasionally. Stir in the garlic, thyme, saffron, and red pepper flakes and cook for 2 minutes.

Add the rice and stir to coat all the grains with butter and oil. Add the wine and cook over medium-low heat, stirring constantly, for 5 minutes, until almost all the liquid has been absorbed. Add ½ cup of the simmering stock to the rice and cook, stirring frequently (see note). When the stock is almost completely absorbed, continue adding stock, ½ cup at a time, simmering the risotto until the stock is absorbed each time before adding more stock. Cook until the rice is al dente; it should take between 25 and 30 minutes.

When the rice is done, stir in the crème fraîche, 2 teaspoons salt, and 1 teaspoon black pepper. Fold in the crabmeat and peas and cook over low heat for 2 minutes, until the crabmeat is warmed through. Add just enough simmering stock to make the risotto moist and creamy. Serve hot in large, shallow bowls and sprinkle with chives and lemon zest.

I use either seafood stock from my fish store or canned Bar Harbor Seafood Stock.

I find that using a ½-cup ladle for the stock makes it easy to see how much to add.

baked rigatoni with lamb ragù

No collection of comfort foods is complete without some kind of baked pasta—it's so satisfying. Instead of the usual lasagna, I made this baked rigatoni with a hearty ragù of lamb, tomatoes, and good red wine. With a little mozzarella and Parmesan baked on top, you've got a dinner that will make everyone happy.

SERVES 8

3 tablespoons good olive oil

1½ cups chopped yellow onion (1 large)

2 cups (½-inch) diced carrots (3 large)

2 cups (½-inch) diced fennel, cored (1 medium)

1 pound ground lamb

1 tablespoon minced garlic (3 cloves)

1 tablespoon whole fennel seeds, roughly chopped

2 tablespoons tomato paste

1 (28-ounce) can crushed tomatoes, such as San Marzano

2½ cups dry red wine, such as Chianti or Côtes du Rhône, divided

1 teaspoon dried oregano, crushed with your hands

¼ teaspoon crushed red pepper flakes

Kosher salt and freshly ground black pepper

1 pound rigatoni, such as De Cecco

2 extra-large eggs

⅔ cup heavy cream

1 pound fresh salted mozzarella, divided

½ cup freshly grated Italian Parmesan cheese

Heat the olive oil in a medium (10 to 11-inch) heavy-bottomed pot or Dutch oven, such as Le Creuset, over medium heat. Add the onion, carrots, and fennel and sauté for 10 minutes, stirring occasionally, until the vegetables begin to brown. Add the lamb, garlic, and fennel seeds and cook for 8 minutes, breaking up the lamb with a wooden spoon, until no longer pink. Stir in the tomato paste, tomatoes, 2 cups of the wine, the oregano, red pepper flakes, 1 tablespoon salt, and 1 teaspoon black pepper. Bring to a boil, lower the heat, and simmer, partly covered, for 40 minutes, stirring occasionally. Off the heat, stir in the remaining ½ cup of red wine.

Preheat the oven to 350 degrees. Bring a large pot of water to a boil, add 2 tablespoons salt and the rigatoni and cook according to the directions on the package, until barely al dente. Drain.

In a large bowl, whisk together the eggs and cream. Add the rigatoni and toss well. Grate half of the mozzarella on a box grater and add it to the rigatoni mixture. Add the lamb mixture, 2 teaspoons salt, and 1 teaspoon black pepper and toss well.

Transfer a 10 × 14 × 2-inch baking dish and sprinkle with the Parmesan. Slice the remaining mozzarella and arrange it on top. Bake for 40 to 45 minutes, until the sauce is hot and bubbling and some of the pasta is crusty on top. Serve hot.

make ahead: *The dish can be completely assembled a day in advance and refrigerated. Bake just before serving.*

spring green spaghetti carbonara

Spaghetti carbonara is true Italian comfort food but it's incredibly rich. I updated it with lots of fresh green vegetables like English peas, snow peas, and asparagus. Instead of blanching the vegetables in a second pot of water, I cook them in the same pot along with the pasta. So easy!

SERVES 6

Kosher salt and freshly ground black pepper

12 ounces spaghetti, such as De Cecco

½ pound snow peas, julienned lengthwise

1 cup shelled fresh peas (1 pound in the pod), or frozen peas

12 to 14 thin asparagus, bottom third discarded and tips sliced in 2-inch pieces

2 tablespoons good olive oil

8 ounces small-diced pancetta (page 104)

½ cup heavy cream

2 extra-large eggs

2 extra-large egg yolks

¾ cup freshly grated Italian Parmesan cheese, plus extra for serving

5 scallions, white and green parts, thinly sliced diagonally

¼ cup minced fresh chives, plus extra for serving

Zest and juice of 1 lemon

Bring a large pot of water with 2 tablespoons salt to a boil. Add the spaghetti and cook for 8 minutes, stirring occasionally. Reserve a cup of the pasta water, then add the snow peas, fresh peas, and asparagus to the spaghetti and cook for 2 minutes longer. Drain the pasta and vegetables together.

Meanwhile, heat the oil in a medium (10 to 11-inch) sauté pan over medium heat, add the pancetta, and cook for 7 to 9 minutes, stirring occasionally, until browned. Transfer the pancetta to a plate lined with paper towels and set aside.

While the pancetta cooks, fill a large bowl with the hottest tap water and set aside to heat the bowl. Just before you drain the pasta, pour the water out of the bowl. Put the cream, eggs, egg yolks, and ¼ cup of the reserved pasta water into the bowl and whisk to combine. Immediately, add the hot pasta and vegetables and toss with tongs for a full minute or two, until the pasta absorbs the sauce. Add enough reserved hot pasta water to keep the sauce creamy. Add the ¾ cup Parmesan, the scallions, chives, lemon zest and juice, 1 tablespoon salt, and 1 teaspoon pepper and toss well. Add the pancetta, sprinkle with salt, and serve hot sprinkled with extra chives and Parmesan.

truffled mac & cheese

Some comfort foods like mac & cheese just never go out of style. Kids love it and so do adults when it's dressed up for company. This dish is particularly good for entertaining because you can assemble it a day in advance and bake it before dinner. Wild mushrooms, truffle butter, and cream sherry make this mac & cheese really special.

SERVES 6 TO 8

2 tablespoons unsalted butter

Good olive oil

½ pound shiitake mushrooms, stems removed, caps sliced ½ inch thick

½ pound cremini mushrooms, stems removed, caps sliced ½ inch thick

¼ cup cream sherry, such as Harveys Bristol Cream

Kosher salt and freshly ground black pepper

1 pound cavatappi pasta, such as De Cecco

4 cups whole milk

3 ounces white truffle butter, such as Urbani (see note)

½ cup all-purpose flour

4 cups grated Gruyère cheese (10 ounces)

3 cups grated extra-sharp white Cheddar (8 ounces)

½ teaspoon ground nutmeg

1½ cups diced white bread, crusts removed

2 garlic cloves, chopped

3 tablespoons chopped fresh parsley

Preheat the oven to 375 degrees.

Heat the butter and 2 tablespoons oil in a large (12-inch) sauté pan, add the mushrooms, and cook over medium heat for 3 to 5 minutes, until tender. Add the sherry and sauté for 2 to 3 minutes, until the sherry is absorbed. Set aside.

Meanwhile, add a tablespoon of salt to a large pot of water and bring to a boil. Add the pasta, cook for 6 to 8 minutes, until al dente, and drain.

Scald the milk in a medium saucepan. Melt the truffle butter in a large (4-quart) saucepan and whisk in the flour. Cook over low heat for 2 minutes, whisking constantly. Slowly add the scalded milk and cook for 2 minutes, stirring with a wooden spoon, until thick and creamy. Off the heat, add the Gruyère, Cheddar, 2 tablespoons salt, 2 teaspoons pepper, and the nutmeg.

In a large bowl, combine the pasta, the cream sauce, and two thirds of the mushrooms and pour into a 10 × 13 × 2-inch ovenproof baking dish. Place the bread, garlic, and parsley in the bowl of a food processor fitted with the steel blade and process to make fine crumbs. Sprinkle the herbed crumbs evenly on the pasta and arrange the remaining mushrooms down the middle.

Bake for 35 to 45 minutes, until the sauce is bubbly and the crumbs are golden brown. Let stand for 5 minutes and serve hot.

You can find white truffle butter at urbani.com; it keeps in the freezer for up to 6 months. Don't substitute black truffle butter; the flavor is very different.

spaghetti squash arrabbiata

Spaghetti squash seems to be everywhere but it doesn't have a lot of flavor on its own. I like to treat it like pasta, as with this baked squash with spicy arrabbiata sauce, fresh mozzarella, and basil. It's all the comforting flavors of chicken parmesan—but vegetarian and gluten-free!

SERVES 4

2 medium spaghetti squashes (about 3 pounds each)

6 tablespoons good olive oil

1½ teaspoons dried oregano, crushed in your hands

Kosher salt and freshly ground black pepper

Arrabbiata Sauce (recipe follows)

8 ounces fresh bocconcini (small mozzarella balls) (see note)

4 tablespoons freshly grated Italian Parmesan cheese

Julienned fresh basil leaves, for garnish

If you can't find bocconcini, you can substitute sliced salted fresh mozzarella.

Preheat the oven to 425 degrees.

Cut each squash in half lengthwise, starting by plunging the tip of a large chef's knife into the side of the squash, then banging the squash and knife on a cutting board to split the squash in half. Remove the seeds and place the squash, cut sides up, on a sheet pan lined with aluminum foil. Divide the olive oil among the 4 halves, then brush the cut sides of the squash with the oil. Sprinkle the squash with the oregano, 4 teaspoons salt, and 1½ teaspoons pepper. Roast for 50 minutes to one hour, until the flesh is tender and the edges are beginning to brown.

Reheat the Arrabbiata Sauce in a large pot. Scoop out almost all the spaghetti squash (leaving a ½-inch border of squash in the shells) and transfer it to the pot with the sauce. Toss well. Spoon the mixture back into the shells and distribute the bocconcini on the 4 squash halves. Sprinkle with the Parmesan and bake for 10 to 12 minutes, until the squash is hot and the bocconcini are melted. Sprinkle with the basil and serve hot.

arrabbiata sauce

Missy Robbins is one of the most astonishing chefs in the country. Her restaurants Lilia and Misi in Brooklyn are two of our favorite restaurants in New York and this sauce is based on one of her amazing pasta sauces. It has a stunning amount of garlic in it but don't worry; the flavor mellows as it cooks.

SERVES 4

⅔ cup good olive oil

1 cup whole peeled garlic cloves (2 to 3 heads of garlic)

2 (28-ounce) cans whole peeled Italian plum tomatoes, preferably San Marzano, drained

2 teaspoons whole fennel seeds, chopped

1 teaspoon crushed red pepper flakes

⅓ cup dry Italian red wine, such as Chianti

Kosher salt and freshly ground black pepper

¼ cup julienned fresh basil leaves

make ahead: *Prepare the arrabbiata sauce and store it covered in the fridge for up to a week.*

In a medium (10 to 11-inch) pot or Dutch oven, such as Le Creuset, warm the olive oil over medium-low heat. Add the garlic and cook for 10 to 12 minutes, tossing occasionally, until the garlic has softened and is lightly browned. Watch it closely so it doesn't burn.

Meanwhile, place the tomatoes in a food processor fitted with the steel blade and pulse until roughly chopped. With a slotted spoon, transfer the garlic to the food processor and pulse again just to chop the garlic.

Pour the tomato mixture into the pot with the oil; add the fennel seeds, red pepper flakes, wine, 1 tablespoon salt, and 1 teaspoon black pepper. Bring to a boil, lower the heat, and simmer for 30 minutes. Off the heat, stir in the basil and taste for seasonings.

vegetables
& sides

roasted broccolini & cheddar

———

fresh zucchini with lemon & mint

———

roasted cauliflower with lemon & capers

———

charred carrots

———

roasted butternut squash with brown butter & sage

———

cheddar & scallion creamed corn

———

roasted shishito peppers with easy hollandaise

———

celery root & cauliflower purée

———

provençal zucchini gratin

———

sautéed rainbow chard

———

emily's english roasted potatoes

———

fresh corn polenta

———

puréed potatoes with lemon

———

outrageous garlic bread

———

roasted sweet potatoes with chipotle orange butter

———

vegetables revisited

Years ago, a friend and I were in San Francisco and I had always wanted to go to Zuni Café, which was owned by the beloved Judy Rodgers. We got into a taxi at the hotel, told the driver where we wanted to go, and he said, "You're going to order the roast chicken and the Caesar salad, right?" LOL! Zuni Café was so famous that even the taxi drivers knew what to order! (That's what we ordered and it was amazing!)

After dinner, Judy kindly sat down with us and I asked her what the most popular dish on the menu was. She replied, "Whatever we pair the buttermilk mashed potatoes with—that station gets slammed that night!" OMG a *side* dish—specifically mashed potatoes with the added tang of buttermilk—was the star on the

menu?! Those potatoes were so appealing that people didn't even care what main course they were served with. And I can attest, they're *that* delicious.

I doubt steamed broccoli with a squeeze of fresh lemon juice is anyone's idea of comfort food. Instead, we gravitate toward old-fashioned dishes like those buttermilk mashed potatoes, updated to taste a little more interesting, more modern. Of course, I had to have a mashed potato recipe in a book about modern comfort food (right?) so I added a whole tablespoon of lemon zest to balance all the cream and butter in my recipe for Puréed Potatoes with Lemon (page 174). It's rich and delicious but that lemony acidic edge makes it more sophisticated so you sit up and take notice. For my Celery Root & Cauliflower Purée (page 165), I mostly used celery root and cauliflower for the purée instead of

potatoes, and added lots of slowly sautéed leeks to give it more depth of flavor. Crispy Brussels sprout leaves on top contrast with the creamy purée underneath. It's rich and delicious.

We have a whole new approach to cooking veggies these days. The vegetables I remember from childhood were boiled or steamed, and sadly almost always overcooked and mushy. In the early 1980s, we started "blanching and shocking" vegetables— putting them in boiling water for maybe thirty seconds and then in ice water to stop the cooking and preserve the bright colors. The vegetables weren't actually *raw* but they weren't completely cooked, either. They were better than overcooked vegetables but not really delicious and comforting. Then in the late '80s, I started roasting vegetables, and I've never looked back. It's so simple: prepped vegetables tossed with olive oil, salt, and pepper on a big sheet pan and into the oven at a high heat so they brown and

caramelize until they're crispy outside and fully cooked inside. My Roasted Broccolini & Cheddar (page 150) roasts in ten minutes, then I sprinkle on big shards of aged Cheddar and throw it back in the oven for a few minutes just to melt the cheese. It has a lot of the same flavors as old-fashioned broccoli with a cheese sauce but you don't have to make a sauce and it's fresher and more delicious!

While I don't automatically think of vegetables as comfort food, they definitely qualify if you give them a little love and attention. Creamy, crispy, and cheesy are all things that make vegetables appealing. As with Judy Rodgers's buttermilk mashed potatoes, you can pair these dishes with a simple roast chicken or fish and you'll have a dinner that will wow your friends and family.

roasted broccolini & cheddar

In the 1950s, cooks used to hide frozen vegetables under some mystery "cheese" sauce. The combination of green vegetables and cheese was a good idea but I prefer roasting broccolini (it's sweeter and more tender than broccoli) and, instead of making a sauce, I simply melt good sharp Cheddar on the broccolini. We love this!

SERVES 4

1½ pounds broccolini

Good olive oil

Kosher salt and freshly ground black pepper

6 ounces good sharp aged white Cheddar, such as Cabot

Juice of ½ lemon

Preheat the oven to 400 degrees.

Remove and discard the bottom half of the broccolini stems. Cut the remaining broccolini stems in half or quarters lengthwise, depending on the size of the stems. Don't cut the florets—just pull them apart. Place the broccolini on a sheet pan. Drizzle 4 tablespoons olive oil on the broccolini and sprinkle with 1 teaspoon salt and ½ teaspoon pepper. Toss well, making sure the broccolini is lightly coated with oil. Spread the broccolini in one layer and roast for 10 minutes, tossing once with a metal spatula, until crisp-tender.

Meanwhile, slice the Cheddar ¼ inch thick and break it into large crumbles. When the broccolini is ready, sprinkle the cheese on the broccolini and return to the oven for 3 to 4 minutes, just until the cheese melts. Squeeze on the lemon juice, taste for seasonings, and serve hot.

fresh zucchini with lemon & mint

This zucchini dish is the simplest no-cook side dish to make in the summer with lemon, mint, and Parmesan. It's easy and delicious with grilled lamb or chicken and you don't even need to turn the oven on.

SERVES 4 TO 6

4 medium zucchini, unpeeled, ends trimmed

Kosher salt and freshly ground black pepper

¼ cup freshly squeezed lemon juice (1 to 2 lemons)

¼ cup good olive oil

3 tablespoons julienned fresh mint leaves

2 tablespoons freshly grated Italian Parmesan cheese

Shaved Italian Parmesan cheese, for serving

Oxo makes an excellent and inexpensive mandoline.

Set a mandoline on the finest julienne setting and cut the zucchini lengthwise in long strands. (If your mandoline doesn't have a hand guard, use a towel to protect your hand.) Place the zucchini in a large colander, toss it with 1 tablespoon salt and set aside to drain for 5 minutes.

Meanwhile, make the vinaigrette: whisk together the lemon juice, olive oil, 1 teaspoon salt, and ½ teaspoon pepper and set aside.

Carefully pat the zucchini dry with paper towels and transfer to a large, shallow serving bowl. Drizzle on enough vinaigrette to moisten. Add 2 tablespoons of the mint and the grated Parmesan and toss well. Sprinkle with pepper, the remaining tablespoon of mint, and shaved Parmesan. Serve at room temperature.

roasted cauliflower with lemon & capers

One of my favorite cookbook authors is David Tanis. He was a chef at Chez Panisse in California and he writes recipes that are simple and flavorful and use ingredients you can find anywhere. This roasted cauliflower is inspired by a recipe in his wonderful book Market Cooking.

SERVES 4

1 large head cauliflower (2½ pounds), green leaves removed

Good olive oil

Kosher salt and freshly ground black pepper

2 tablespoons unsalted butter

3 anchovies, minced

2 teaspoons minced garlic (2 cloves)

Zest and juice of 1 lemon, plus extra juice for serving

¼ teaspoon crushed red pepper flakes

1 tablespoon capers, drained and roughly chopped

2 tablespoons freshly grated Italian Parmesan cheese

Whole fresh flat-leaf parsley leaves

You want straight-cut edges on the cauliflower so it will brown on the sheet pan.

Preheat the oven to 450 degrees.

Cut the cauliflower in half through the core and cut out the core. Place the cut sides down on a board and cut ¾-inch-thick slices (see note). Break the slices into large pieces and place them on a sheet pan with 4 tablespoons olive oil, 1 teaspoon salt, and 1 teaspoon black pepper. Toss well. Roast for 25 to 30 minutes, until tender and browned, carefully turning once.

Meanwhile, heat the butter and 2 tablespoons olive oil in a small saucepan over medium heat. Add the anchovies and cook for one minute, breaking them up as they cook. Add the garlic and cook for one minute. Off the heat, add the lemon zest, lemon juice, red pepper flakes, and capers.

To serve, transfer the cauliflower to a serving platter. Drizzle on the sauce, then sprinkle with the Parmesan, a squeeze of lemon juice, and the parsley. Serve warm.

charred carrots

One of the things I've explored for this book is remembered flavors. What makes us nostalgic for a particular comfort food? My friend Eli Zabar thinks "burnt" is one of those remembered flavors, as when your mother burnt the roast! Charring carrots under a broiler brings out their sweetness so they taste and smell like real home cooking.

SERVES 4

1½ pounds rainbow carrots, tops removed, unpeeled and scrubbed

Good olive oil

1½ teaspoons minced fresh thyme leaves

Kosher salt and freshly ground black pepper

Zest and juice of ½ orange

1 tablespoon syrupy balsamic vinegar (see note)

Fleur de sel or sea salt

Balsamic vinegar comes in different strengths, with older, more aged vinegars being more concentrated and syrupy. Use a small amount of aged vinegar so it doesn't overpower the sweet carrots. Be sure the only ingredient in your vinegar is "grape must" so you know it's the real thing.

Position an oven rack 4 inches below the broiler and preheat the broiler.

If you're using baby rainbow carrots, cut them in half lengthwise. Otherwise, cut the carrots crosswise in 4-inch lengths. Cut the larger pieces lengthwise in half or quarters to roughly make 4 × ½-inch sticks. Place the carrots on a sheet pan, drizzle them with 3 tablespoons olive oil, and sprinkle with the thyme, 1½ teaspoons kosher salt, and ½ teaspoon pepper. Toss with your hands and spread out in one layer.

Broil the carrots for 8 to 10 minutes, tossing every few minutes with a large metal spatula, until they are tender and randomly charred (I prop the oven door open a little so the broiler doesn't turn off). Sprinkle the carrots with the orange zest and orange juice. Drizzle lightly with the balsamic vinegar, sprinkle with some fleur de sel, taste for seasonings, and serve warm or at room temperature.

roasted butternut squash with brown butter & sage

This is another recipe adapted from David Tanis's cookbook Market Cooking. *Butternut squash is my favorite vegetable and I could make this dish every day. It's somehow both comforting and good for you at the same time—roasted butternut squash drizzled with brown butter, fresh sage, red pepper flakes, and lemon. It's an amazing combination of flavors!*

SERVES 4

2 pounds butternut squash

2 tablespoons good olive oil

Kosher salt and freshly ground black pepper

3 tablespoons unsalted butter

1 tablespoon chopped fresh sage leaves

⅛ teaspoon crushed red pepper flakes

Finely grated lemon zest

Preheat the oven to 400 degrees.

Peel the butternut squash and halve it lengthwise. Remove and discard the seeds and slice the squash crosswise ½ inch thick. Place the squash on a sheet pan, drizzle with the olive oil, and sprinkle with 1 teaspoon salt and ½ teaspoon black pepper. Toss together and spread out the slices in one layer. Roast for 25 to 30 minutes, tossing occasionally, until browned and tender.

Meanwhile, melt the butter in a small (8-inch) sauté pan over medium heat. Add the sage, red pepper flakes, ¼ teaspoon salt, and ¼ teaspoon black pepper and cook for 2 to 3 minutes, swirling often until the butter begins to brown and has a nutty aroma. Remove from the heat.

Place the squash on a serving plate. Gently reheat the brown butter and spoon it over the squash. Lightly sprinkle some lemon zest on top, sprinkle with salt, and serve hot.

cheddar & scallion creamed corn

When I was a kid, my mother used to heat up creamed corn from a can—not my favorite side dish. Now, I buy sweet corn from a farm stand and make the real thing: sautéed corn with half-and-half, Cheddar, and Parmesan cheese.

SERVES 6

6 tablespoons (¾ stick) unsalted butter

2 cups thinly sliced scallions, white and green parts (12 to 14 scallions)

6 cups fresh corn kernels cut off the cob (8 to 10 ears) (see note)

Kosher salt and freshly ground black pepper

⅔ cup half-and-half

2 cups grated extra-sharp white Cheddar, such as Cabot (5 ounces)

2 tablespoons freshly grated Italian Parmesan cheese

In a large (12-inch) sauté pan or medium (10 to 11-inch) Dutch oven, such as Le Creuset, melt the butter over medium heat. Add the scallions and cook for 2 minutes, stirring occasionally. Add the corn, 1½ teaspoons salt, and ¾ teaspoon pepper and cook over medium-high heat, stirring occasionally, for 4 to 6 minutes (depending on the tenderness of the corn), until the corn is just cooked through.

Transfer 2 cups of the mixture to a food processor fitted with the steel blade. Add the half-and-half and process until coarsely puréed. Pour the mixture back into the pan, bring to a simmer, and cook for 3 minutes, stirring occasionally, until thickened. Off the heat, stir in the Cheddar and Parmesan, sprinkle with salt, and serve hot.

To cut kernels of corn, remove the stem end of the ear with a sharp knife, stand it on a clean kitchen towel, and run the knife between the kernels and the cob. To transfer the corn to the pan, lift the towel and pour in the kernels.

roasted shishito peppers with easy hollandaise

You could put Hollandaise sauce on anything and turn it into comfort food. It's often served on asparagus but I had some shishito peppers, which I roasted and served with Hollandaise. I love the mild heat from the peppers with the sharp lemon and butter. And I make the Hollandaise in the microwave, so it's the easiest Hollandaise ever!

SERVES 4

1 pound shishito peppers

Good olive oil

Kosher salt and freshly ground black pepper

3 extra-large egg yolks

3 tablespoons freshly squeezed lemon juice

2 pinches cayenne pepper

8 tablespoons (1 stick) unsalted butter, melted

Preheat the oven to 400 degrees.

Place the shishito peppers on a sheet pan with 2 tablespoons olive oil, 1 teaspoon salt, and ½ teaspoon black pepper. Toss the peppers to coat them with oil, spread them out in one layer, and roast for 10 to 12 minutes, until tender but still bright green.

While the peppers are roasting, whisk the egg yolks, lemon juice, cayenne pepper, and ¾ teaspoon salt together in a medium microwave-safe bowl. Slowly pour in the melted butter, whisking constantly. Microwave the mixture on high for 15 seconds. Remove the bowl from the microwave and whisk again. Continue microwaving and whisking in 10-second increments, just until the mixture is thickened and smooth like mayonnaise. Taste for seasonings.

Serve the shishito peppers with the Hollandaise on the side for dipping.

celery root & cauliflower purée

Everyone's ultimate comfort food is mashed potatoes so I'm always looking for alternatives that are equally comforting. This purée is as creamy and delicious as mashed potatoes but has so much more flavor. The crispy Brussels sprout leaves on the creamy purée make a satisfying contrast in texture.

SERVES 6 TO 8

Good olive oil

3 tablespoons unsalted butter, divided

2½ cups chopped leeks, white and light green parts (2 leeks) (page 58)

2 pounds celery root, peeled and ½-inch diced (see note)

1 pound cauliflower, core removed, cut into florets

8 ounces Yukon Gold potatoes, peeled and ½-inch diced

Kosher salt and freshly ground black pepper

3 cups half-and-half

8 Brussels sprouts

Preheat the oven to 400 degrees.

Heat 1 tablespoon olive oil and 2 tablespoons of the butter in a large pot or Dutch oven, such as Le Creuset. Add the leeks and sauté over medium heat for 3 to 5 minutes, until tender. Add the celery root, cauliflower, potatoes, 1 tablespoon salt, and 1 teaspoon pepper. Sauté the vegetables for 4 to 5 minutes, stirring occasionally, until they begin to soften. Add the half-and-half, bring to boil, lower the heat, cover, and simmer for 15 minutes, stirring occasionally, until the vegetables are tender.

Meanwhile, core the Brussels sprouts and pull off the outer green leaves, saving the inner white leaves for another use. Place the leaves on a sheet pan, add 2 tablespoons olive oil and 1 teaspoon salt, and toss with your hands. Spread out in one layer and roast for 10 minutes, until the leaves are lightly browned and crispy.

Transfer the celery root mixture to a food processor fitted with the steel blade and process until coarsely puréed. Return the mixture to the pot, add the remaining 1 tablespoon of butter along with 2 teaspoons salt and 1 teaspoon pepper, and reheat. Transfer the hot purée to a serving dish, drizzle with oil, and sprinkle with crispy Brussels sprouts leaves. Serve hot.

The trick to cutting a hard root vegetable like celery root without a trip to the hospital is to cut off the bottom with a knife so it stands up solidly before you remove the peel with the knife. Cut the vegetable in half and place the cut side down on the board before dicing.

provençal zucchini gratin

Richard Olney was a curmudgeonly but extraordinary cook who wrote about Provençal cooking at the same time Julia Child was teaching Americans how to make classic French dishes. Olney's iconic book Lulu's Provençal Table *was about his friend Madame Peyraud, whom everyone called Lulu. I've loved zucchini gratins since I wrote a recipe for one in my* Barefoot in Paris *cookbook—but this one is even better.*

SERVES 4 TO 6

5 tablespoons unsalted butter, divided, plus extra for the dish

1 large yellow onion, halved and sliced crosswise

2½ pounds small zucchini, sliced ½ inch thick crosswise

Kosher salt and freshly ground black pepper

1 tablespoon all-purpose flour

1 cup half-and-half

2 teaspoons minced fresh thyme leaves

¼ teaspoon ground nutmeg

¾ cup ground fresh bread crumbs from a boule, crusts removed

¾ cup grated Gruyère cheese (2 ounces)

Preheat the oven to 425 degrees. Butter an 8 × 10-inch oval gratin dish.

In a medium (10 to 11-inch) pot or Dutch oven, heat 3 tablespoons of the butter over medium-low heat. Add the onion and cook for 10 to 15 minutes, stirring occasionally, until tender but not browned. Add the zucchini and 2 teaspoons salt, cover, and cook for 15 minutes. Uncover and cook, stirring occasionally, for another 10 minutes, until the zucchini is tender but not falling apart.

Sprinkle the zucchini mixture with the flour and stir gently. Raise the heat to medium-high and slowly add the half-and-half, allowing each addition to come to a boil while you're adding it. Off the heat, stir in the thyme, nutmeg, 1 teaspoon salt, and ½ teaspoon pepper.

Spoon the mixture into the prepared dish and lightly flatten the top. Combine the bread crumbs and Gruyère in a small bowl and sprinkle on top. Cut the remaining 2 tablespoons of butter in small dice and sprinkle on top. Bake for 20 minutes, until the top is browned and the gratin is bubbly. Allow to sit for 10 minutes and serve hot or warm.

sautéed
rainbow chard

I was looking for a quick vegetable to serve with chicken for dinner one night and realized I had a lot of rainbow chard in the garden. Happily, it's available in grocery stores everywhere now. I sauté the stems first and then cook the leaves with garlic, salt, and pepper. A sprinkling of Parmesan at the end makes everything taste even better!

SERVES 4

2 pounds rainbow chard, washed, with some water still on the leaves

2 tablespoons good olive oil

2 tablespoons minced garlic (6 cloves)

Kosher salt and freshly ground black pepper

¼ cup grated Italian Parmesan cheese

Remove the chard stems from the leaves and cut the stems crosswise in 1-inch pieces. Tear or cut the greens in large pieces and set aside.

In a large (12-inch) sauté pan, heat the olive oil over medium heat until it's sizzling. Add the stems and cook for 4 to 5 minutes, until tender. Add the garlic, 1 teaspoon salt, and ½ teaspoon pepper and cook for just one minute.

Add a big handful of the leaves to the pan and cook over medium-high heat, tossing with tongs, until wilted enough to accommodate more leaves in the pan. Continue adding and tossing until all the leaves are added and just barely cooked. Off the heat, sprinkle with the Parmesan, taste for seasonings, and serve warm.

emily's english roasted potatoes

The adorable and talented Emily Blunt came to film an episode of Barefoot Contessa *with me when her fabulous movie* Mary Poppins Returns *debuted in theaters. We prepared a proper English Sunday lunch together and she showed me how to make her family's roasted potatoes. She describes them as crispy on the outside and creamy inside, which is exactly what they are! Yum!!*

SERVES 6 TO 8

Kosher salt

3 pounds large Yukon Gold potatoes, peeled and 1½ to 2-inch diced

½ cup vegetable oil

Coarse sea salt or fleur de sel

Minced fresh parsley

Preheat the oven to 425 degrees.

Bring a large pot of water with 2 tablespoons kosher salt to a boil. Add the potatoes, return to a boil, lower the heat, and simmer for 8 minutes. Drain the potatoes, place them back in the pot with the lid on, and shake the pot roughly for 5 seconds to rough up the edges. Carefully transfer the potatoes in one layer to a baking rack set over a sheet pan. Set aside to dry for at least 15 minutes. (They can sit uncovered at room temperature for several hours or in the fridge for up to 6 hours.)

Pour the oil onto another sheet pan, tilt the pan to distribute the oil, and place the pan in the oven for 5 to 7 minutes, until the oil is smoking hot. Transfer the potatoes *carefully* into the oil (I use a large metal spatula) and toss them lightly to coat each potato with the hot oil. Evenly spread out the potatoes and lower the oven temperature to 350 degrees F. Roast for 45 minutes to one hour, turning the potatoes occasionally with tongs, until very browned and crisp on the outside and tender and creamy inside.

Transfer to a serving platter, sprinkle generously with 1½ to 2 teaspoons sea salt and parsley and serve hot.

fresh corn polenta

In the category of comfort food, polenta is right up there with chicken soup and mashed potatoes. I've revisited my classic polenta by adding fresh sautéed corn, which gives both flavor and texture to the polenta. It's amazing served with Roasted Sausages, Peppers & Onions (page 121) or even on its own with a simple roast chicken.

SERVES 6

3 cups chicken stock, preferably homemade (page 64)

1½ teaspoons minced garlic (2 cloves)

¾ cup fine cornmeal, such as Indian Head

Kosher salt and freshly ground black pepper

4 tablespoons (½ stick) unsalted butter

3 cups fresh corn kernels cut off the cobs (4 large ears)

½ cup freshly grated Italian Parmesan cheese

2 tablespoons crème fraîche

Combine the chicken stock, ½ cup water, and the garlic in a large saucepan and bring to a full boil over high heat. Slowly add the cornmeal while whisking constantly to ensure there are no lumps. Switch to a wooden spoon, add 1½ teaspoons salt and 1 teaspoon pepper, and simmer over low heat for 15 minutes, stirring often, until the polenta is thick but still creamy. (The timing will depend on the cornmeal that you choose.) Be sure to scrape the bottom of the pan with the wooden spoon so the bottom doesn't burn.

Meanwhile, heat the butter in a large (12-inch) sauté pan over medium heat. Add the corn and cook for 5 to 8 minutes, depending on the starchiness of the corn, until the corn is cooked through and starting to brown around the edge of the pan.

Off the heat, stir the corn, Parmesan, and crème fraîche into the polenta. Taste for seasonings and serve hot.

make ahead: *Prepare the polenta completely and refrigerate for up to a few days. Spoon into a saucepan with extra chicken stock or water and reheat over low heat until creamy and hot.*

puréed potatoes with lemon

There's an Argentinean restaurant in Paris that serves the most amazing steaks plus puréed potatoes you can order with truffles, chimichurri, or lemon. I particularly love the lemon ones because the acidity balances the richness of the steak and potatoes. This is truly updated comfort food.

SERVES 4 TO 6

2½ pounds large Yukon Gold potatoes

Kosher salt and freshly ground black pepper

½ pound (2 sticks) cold unsalted butter

1 cup whole milk

1 tablespoon grated lemon zest (2 lemons)

make ahead: *Lemon gets bitter as it sits so these potatoes are best served the day they're made. Prepare them completely without the zest and set them aside at room temperature. Reheat in a bowl set over a pan of simmering water, adding warm milk, as needed, until the texture is right. Whisk in the lemon zest just before serving.*

Peel the potatoes and cut them in 1½ to 2-inch chunks. Place the potatoes in a large saucepan, add water to cover by one inch, and add 2 tablespoons salt. Cover, bring to a boil, lower the heat, and simmer uncovered for 15 minutes, until the potatoes are very tender when pierced with a small paring knife. Drain and set aside.

Meanwhile, cut the butter in ½-inch dice and put it back in the refrigerator.

After the potatoes are drained, pour the milk into a small saucepan set over low heat and heat the milk *just* until it simmers. Turn off the heat.

Place a food mill fitted with the finest blade on top of the large saucepan. Process the potatoes into the pan. With the heat on low, vigorously whisk in the cold butter several bits at a time, waiting for each addition to be incorporated before adding more butter. When all the butter is added, slowly whisk in enough of the hot milk to make the potatoes the desired consistency—creamy but still thick. Add 2 teaspoons salt and 1 teaspoon pepper. Whisk in the lemon zest, sprinkle with salt, taste for seasonings, and serve hot.

outrageous garlic bread

Garlic bread from the 1960s was usually soft, doughy Italian bread dripping with garlic butter. I've taken a fresh look at it and made the ultimate garlic bread by slathering a crusty baguette with lots of slow-cooked garlic, Parmesan, parsley, and lemon zest and baking it until it's beautifully browned on top. It's so good!

SERVES 8

12 tablespoons (1½ sticks) unsalted butter

1 head garlic, cloves separated and peeled (see note)

1 cup freshly grated Italian Parmesan cheese

2 tablespoons minced fresh parsley

2 teaspoons grated lemon zest

¼ teaspoon crushed red pepper flakes

Kosher salt and freshly ground black pepper

1 (20 to 24-inch-long) crusty French baguette

Fleur de sel or sea salt

Preheat the oven to 450 degrees. (Make sure your oven is clean or it will smoke!)

Melt the butter in a small saucepan over low heat. Add the garlic, stir to coat with the butter, and cook, covered, for 20 minutes, stirring occasionally, until the garlic is very tender. Transfer to a small bowl and set aside until cool enough to handle. Mash the garlic in the butter with a fork. Stir in the Parmesan, parsley, lemon zest, red pepper flakes, 1½ teaspoons kosher salt, and ½ teaspoon black pepper.

Slice the baguette in half lengthwise and place both halves, cut sides up, on a cutting board. Score each half diagonally (don't cut all the way through) in large serving-size pieces. Spoon all of the garlic mixture generously on the cut sides of the bread. Cut each half of the baguette in half crosswise along a score and place the 4 pieces on a sheet pan lined with parchment paper.

Bake for 5 to 7 minutes, until the topping is bubbly and starting to brown and the bread is crisp. Transfer to a board, cut in serving pieces along the scores, sprinkle with fleur de sel, and serve warm.

Peel the garlic by smashing each clove lightly on a board with a chef's knife or place the cloves in a small pot of boiling water for 15 to 30 seconds and the peels will come right off.

make ahead: *Prepare the garlic mixture up to 3 days ahead and refrigerate. Warm it slightly in a microwave to make it just spreadable, then prepare and bake the bread just before serving.*

roasted sweet potatoes with chipotle orange butter

Flavored butters are a great way to bump up the flavor of not just fish or chicken but also simple vegetables. I keep a log of chipotle orange butter in the fridge so I can throw a few sweet potatoes in the oven and have a quick side dish that's good enough to serve to company.

SERVES 6

6 small sweet potatoes (see note)

¼ pound (1 stick) unsalted butter, at room temperature

2 tablespoons pure maple syrup

1 tablespoon minced canned chipotle pepper (in adobo sauce)

1 tablespoon adobo sauce (from the can)

½ teaspoon grated orange zest

Kosher salt and freshly ground black pepper

Choose potatoes that are about the same size so they cook in the same amount of time.

make ahead: *Prepare the chipotle butter and refrigerate for up to a week. Bake the potatoes before serving.*

Preheat the oven to 400 degrees. Line a sheet pan with aluminum foil.

Pierce the potatoes in several places with a sharp knife to prevent them from exploding in the oven. Place the potatoes on the prepared sheet pan and roast for one hour, until they are very tender when pierced with a knife.

Meanwhile, in the bowl of an electric mixer fitted with the paddle attachment, combine the butter, maple syrup, chipotle pepper, adobo sauce, orange zest, 1 teaspoon salt, and ½ teaspoon black pepper on medium speed until well mixed. Cut a 12 × 8-inch piece of parchment paper and place it on a board with the 12-inch edge near you. With a rubber spatula, transfer the butter to the parchment paper, forming a strip along the edge. Using the parchment paper, roll the butter up and away from you to form a log. Refrigerate for at least 15 minutes.

Cut a slit in the top of each potato and squeeze the ends together to open the potatoes. Sprinkle them with salt and black pepper. Cut the chipotle butter in 12 pieces and place 2 pieces in the opening of each potato. Serve hot.

dessert

peach almond torte

———

english lemon posset

———

milk chocolate oreo ice cream

———

black & white cookies

———

bittersweet chocolate cake

———

applesauce cake with bourbon raisins

———

salted pistachio meringues

———

berries & jam milkshakes

———

boston cream pie

———

CONTINUES »

banana rum trifle

———

giant crinkled chocolate chip cookies

———

coffee chocolate chip ice cream sandwiches

———

white chocolate toffee

———

tuscan baked apples

———

chocolate-dipped brown sugar shortbread

———

the evolution of a recipe

Every recipe that I create has a story. Some I nail on the first try, some take a little bit more experimenting—and then there's the occasional recipe that I come back to again and again until I'm finally happy with the results. The ultimate example of this process is my recipe for Boston Cream Pie (page 205), which has literally taken me *years* to get just right.

Boston Cream Pie is actually not a pie at all—it's a cake! It's one of those beloved old-fashioned American desserts. I have to say, when I first made it, I wondered what all the fuss was about. Traditionally, Boston Cream Pie is a vanilla layer cake with vanilla cream filling and a chocolate glaze. It's layers of sweet-on-sweet-on-sweet—perfectly fine but not that kind of *wow!* dessert that I'm always looking for.

I decided that the cake could be so much more sophisticated if I introduced an orange note to both the cake and the pastry cream: it would add complexity without much more work. First, I put orange zest into the cake to give it great flavor. Next, I added Grand Marnier orange liqueur and Cognac to the pastry cream to cut the richness and give it that little "grown-up" edge. Finally, I made the chocolate glaze with a combination of bittersweet and semisweet chocolates so that the chocolate was complex and not too sweet.

When I had made each component the best I could, I assembled my Boston Cream Pie—but sadly, the result was disappointing. The assertive chocolate overpowered the orange in the cake and the thin pastry cream oozed out from between the layers. Ugh. Back to the drawing board! For a week, I baked one cake after another but I was never satisfied. Eventually, I couldn't look at another Boston Cream Pie, so I put the whole thing away to try another time.

A few years ago, while I happened to be working on the recipe again, Christina Tosi, the extraordinary baker who is the founder and owner of Milk Bar, interviewed me for an event at Barnes & Noble in New York City. She asked me if there was a recipe that had eluded me. "Funny you should ask!" I said, "I've been working on Boston Cream Pie for years! I've got the cake right, the pastry cream right, and the chocolate glaze right. But when I put the three of them together, I find that the orange flavor in the cake needs to be a little more assertive." Christina suggested what she called a "soak"—a syrupy glaze that you brush on the cake to give it lots of flavor that also keeps it moist. What a great idea!! The next day I came home and made a sugar syrup with freshly squeezed orange juice and Grand Marnier that I brushed on the cake, and *voilà*! The Boston Cream Pie was FINALLY done. Moist, flavorful, balanced, and totally over the top, it was exactly the Boston Cream Pie of my dreams. I can't wait for you to try it!!

peach almond torte

This recipe is inspired by a famous plum torte by Marian Burros, which the New York Times *published every September for seven years in a row because it was so beloved by readers. Peaches instead of plums and a bit of Grand Marnier give it a whole new spin. This is the easiest cake ever!*

SERVES 6

¾ pound ripe peaches, unpeeled, cut in 8 to 10 wedges (2 large)

2 tablespoons Grand Marnier

¼ pound (1 stick) unsalted butter, at room temperature

¾ cup granulated sugar

½ teaspoon pure vanilla extract

¼ teaspoon pure almond extract

2 extra-large eggs, at room temperature

1 cup all-purpose flour

1 teaspoon baking powder

½ teaspoon kosher salt

2 tablespoons turbinado sugar, such as Sugar in the Raw

2 tablespoons blanched, sliced almonds

Confectioners' sugar

Preheat the oven to 350 degrees. Grease an 8-inch round springform pan.

In a small bowl, combine the peaches with the Grand Marnier and set aside.

In the bowl of an electric mixer fitted with the paddle attachment, cream the butter and granulated sugar on medium speed for 2 minutes, until light and fluffy. With the mixer on low, add the vanilla, almond extract, and eggs, one at a time, scraping down the bowl with a rubber spatula. In a separate bowl, combine the flour, baking powder, and salt. With the mixer on low, slowly add the dry ingredients and mix just until incorporated. Stir with a rubber spatula.

Transfer the batter to the prepared pan and smooth the top. Arrange the peaches, cut sides up, in concentric circles on top. Sprinkle with the turbinado sugar and almonds. Bake for 45 to 50 minutes, until the top is browned and a toothpick inserted in the center comes out clean. Cool slightly, dust with confectioners' sugar, and serve warm or at room temperature.

english lemon posset

Puddings are the essence of comfort food but I was looking for something a little more sophisticated than the usual chocolate or butterscotch. Lemon posset is a charming name for a delicious old-fashioned English lemon pudding, which I've tweaked with limoncello liqueur. This is crazy easy to make!

SERVES 6

3 cups heavy cream

1 cup plus 2 tablespoons sugar, divided

1 tablespoon grated lemon zest (2 to 3 lemons) (see note)

¼ teaspoon kosher salt

⅓ cup freshly squeezed lemon juice

4 tablespoons limoncello liqueur, divided

1 cup fresh raspberries

1 cup sliced fresh strawberries

Zest the lemons with a rasp. Cold, firm lemons are easier to zest than soft ones.

make ahead: *Chill the custards, then cover each one with plastic wrap, and refrigerate for up to 3 days. Prepare the berries before serving.*

Combine the cream, 1 cup of the sugar, the lemon zest, and the salt in a medium (6-inch-round × 5-inch-high) saucepan. (Don't use a smaller pan!) Bring to a boil over medium-high heat, stirring with a wooden spoon to dissolve the sugar. Lower the heat to a vigorous simmer and cook for 6 minutes, without stirring at all. Watch the mixture carefully so it doesn't boil over! If it begins to boil up, take the pan off the heat for a few seconds and then continue to simmer.

Off the heat, stir in the lemon juice and 2 tablespoons of the limoncello and set aside for 20 minutes. Strain the mixture through a fine-mesh sieve into a 4-cup glass measuring cup, pressing on the zest with a rubber spatula. Discard the zest. Divide the cream mixture evenly among six 8 to 10-ounce dessert bowls or glasses and refrigerate uncovered for 3 hours, until firm.

Thirty minutes before serving, prepare the berries. Combine the raspberries, strawberries, the remaining 2 tablespoons of sugar, and the remaining 2 tablespoons of limoncello in a medium bowl and allow to macerate for 30 minutes. To serve, spoon the berries and the juices onto the custards and serve.

milk chocolate oreo ice cream

There is such good ice cream available now that it's rarely worth making your own. This is one of those exceptions. I started with David Lebovitz's Milk Chocolate Ice Cream in his wonderful book The Perfect Scoop *and went on from there. OMG. I actually had to hide this from myself in the back of the freezer so I wouldn't keep eating it all day!*

MAKES 1 QUART

1½ cups heavy cream

8 ounces milk chocolate, such as Green & Black's, finely chopped

2 tablespoons cocoa powder, such as Valrhona

1 teaspoon pure vanilla extract

2 teaspoons Cognac or brandy

1½ cups whole milk

¾ cup sugar

½ teaspoon kosher salt

4 extra-large egg yolks

½ teaspoon cornstarch

2 cups Oreo cookies, roughly chopped (15 cookies)

Place the cream and chocolate in a large heatproof bowl set over a pan of simmering water, making sure the water doesn't touch the bottom of the bowl. Heat *just* until the chocolate melts, stirring occasionally. Off the heat, whisk in the cocoa powder, vanilla, and Cognac and set aside.

In a medium (4½-inch-diameter × 6-inch-high) saucepan over medium heat, heat the milk, sugar, and salt until hot but not simmering. In a separate large bowl, whisk together the egg yolks and cornstarch. Slowly whisk the hot milk mixture into the egg mixture, then pour it back into the saucepan. Cook over medium-low heat for a few minutes, stirring almost constantly with a wooden spoon, until the mixture thickens like heavy cream. (Don't allow it to boil!) Cook for 30 seconds, scraping the bottom of the pan with the spoon. The mixture should coat the spoon and if you run your finger down the back of the spoon, it will leave a clear trail.

Immediately, pour the mixture through a fine-mesh sieve into the chocolate mixture and stir to combine. Cover and chill completely in the fridge or over a bowl of ice water. Transfer to an ice cream maker and freeze according to the manufacturer's instructions. Mix in the Oreos in the last few minutes. Transfer to a container or loaf pan, cover, and freeze. Soften slightly, scoop, and serve frozen.

black & white cookies

Black and white cookies came to New York City with immigrants from Eastern Europe. They're actually more like tender little cakes than cookies and they're always iced with vanilla and chocolate frosting. Be sure to turn them over and glaze the flat bottoms, not the rounded tops. These are my favorite black and white cookies ever!

MAKES 10 LARGE COOKIES

10 tablespoons (1¼ sticks) unsalted butter, at room temperature

1 cup granulated sugar

1 extra-large egg, at room temperature

2 teaspoons pure vanilla extract

1¾ cups all-purpose flour

½ teaspoon baking powder

¼ teaspoon baking soda

½ teaspoon kosher salt

⅓ cup sour cream

FOR THE GLAZES:

4 tablespoons (½ stick) unsalted butter

5 ounces good semisweet chocolate, such as Lindt, roughly chopped

½ teaspoon instant coffee granules, such as Nescafé

2 cups sifted confectioners' sugar

2 tablespoons light corn syrup

½ teaspoon pure vanilla extract

2 to 3 tablespoons heavy cream

Preheat the oven to 350 degrees. Arrange two racks evenly spaced in the oven.

Put the butter and granulated sugar in the bowl of an electric mixer fitted with the paddle attachment and beat on medium-high speed for 2 to 3 minutes, until light and fluffy. With the mixer on low, add the egg and vanilla and mix well, scraping down the sides with a rubber spatula. Sift the flour, baking powder, baking soda, and salt into a bowl. With the mixer on low, alternately add the flour mixture and sour cream in thirds and mix just until combined. Stir with a rubber spatula.

With a standard (2¼-inch) ice cream scoop, place 5 level scoops of batter 2 inches apart on each of two sheet pans lined with parchment paper. Bake for 10 minutes, then rotate and switch the pans from the top to bottom rack to bake the cookies evenly. Bake for another 6 to 8 minutes, until the edges are lightly browned and a cake tester comes out clean. Don't overbake them! Cool on the pans for 5 minutes, then transfer to a wire rack set over a sheet pan to cool completely.

For the chocolate glaze, place the butter, chocolate, and coffee in a heatproof bowl and microwave on high for 30 seconds. Stir the mixture and continue to microwave in 30-second increments until the chocolate is almost melted, allowing the residual heat to finish melting the chocolate completely. Stir the mixture vigorously, until smooth. Turn the cookies so the flat side is up. Hold the cookie in your hand and, with a spoon, carefully pour the chocolate glaze on half of the cookie, forming a straight line down the middle. Allow the glaze to set for 30 minutes.

For the vanilla glaze, whisk together the confectioners' sugar, corn syrup, vanilla, and 2 tablespoons of the cream, adding drops of cream until the glaze is smooth, thick, and barely pourable. Holding the cookie in your hand, with a spoon, pour the white glaze over the unglazed half of each cookie right up to the chocolate glaze. You can smooth it out with an offset spatula, if you need to. Allow to set for 30 minutes. Serve at room temperature.

Instead of using a sifter, I place dry ingredients in a coarse wire strainer set over a bowl and tap the side of the strainer with my hand.

bittersweet chocolate cake

I'm always looking for a new chocolate cake because everyone loves them. I came across a recipe for a French balois, *which is something between a chocolate torte and a molten chocolate cake. This cake will puff up when it bakes and fall back as it cools. It's a rich and elegant dessert.*

SERVES 8

15 tablespoons unsalted butter, plus extra to grease the pan

7 ounces bittersweet chocolate, such as Lindt, broken

1 cup sugar

4 extra-large eggs, lightly beaten

½ teaspoon instant coffee granules, such as Nescafé

½ teaspoon kosher salt

¼ cup all-purpose flour, plus extra for the pan

Sweetened Whipped Cream (page 196), vanilla ice cream, or crème fraîche, for serving

The baking time of this cake is sensitive to the pan size and no two 8-inch pans are exactly the same. Start checking the cake after 25 minutes.

Preheat the oven to 350 degrees. Butter and flour an 8-inch springform pan.

Place a large heatproof bowl over a pot of simmering water, making sure the water doesn't touch the bowl. Put the butter and chocolate in the bowl, stirring occasionally, until the chocolate melts. Take the bowl off the heat and set aside.

First, whisk the sugar into the chocolate mixture, then whisk in the eggs, coffee, and salt, whisking until the mixture is combined and smooth. Sprinkle on the flour and fold it in with a rubber spatula until it's incorporated.

Pour the batter into the prepared pan and place it on a sheet pan. Bake for 30 to 40 minutes (see note), until the top puffs up and cracks and the cake doesn't wobble when you jiggle the pan. (A toothpick will *not* come out clean.) Remove from the oven and cool completely on a baking rack. The cake will deflate as it cools. Run a small knife around the cake and remove the sides of the pan. Cut the cake in wedges and serve warm or at room temperature with Sweetened Whipped Cream, vanilla ice cream, or crème fraîche.

sweetened
whipped cream

MAKES 2 CUPS

1 cup cold heavy cream

1 tablespoon sugar

1 teaspoon pure vanilla extract

Pour the cream into the bowl of an electric mixer
fitted with the whisk attachment. Add the sugar
and vanilla and beat on high speed until the cream
forms soft peaks.

bourbon
cream cheese frosting

6 ounces cream cheese, at room temperature

6 tablespoons (¾ stick) unsalted butter, at room temperature

1 tablespoon good bourbon, such as Maker's Mark

½ teaspoon pure vanilla extract

½ pound confectioners' sugar, sifted (see note)

Place the cream cheese, butter, bourbon, and vanilla in the bowl of an electric mixer fitted with the paddle attachment and beat on medium speed until smooth. With the mixer on low, slowly add the sugar and mix well. Scrape down the sides and stir well with a rubber spatula.

One-half pound of sifted confectioners' sugar is about 2 cups plus 2 tablespoons.

applesauce cake with bourbon raisins

I love the earthiness of old-fashioned cakes but I often wish they had more flavor. Apples and raisins are great together in a cake but I thought some bourbon would give it more depth, so I infused the raisins with bourbon before adding them to the batter. A splash of bourbon in the cream cheese frosting didn't hurt either.

MAKES ONE 9-INCH ROUND
CAKE / SERVES 8

¾ cup golden raisins

2 tablespoons good bourbon, such as Maker's Mark

10 tablespoons (1¼ sticks) unsalted butter, at room temperature, plus extra to grease the pan

¾ cup granulated sugar

¾ cup light brown sugar, lightly packed

2 teaspoons pure vanilla extract

2 extra-large eggs, at room temperature

1¾ cups all-purpose flour, plus extra for the pan

1½ teaspoons baking soda

1 teaspoon ground cinnamon

¼ teaspoon ground nutmeg

¼ teaspoon ground cloves

1 teaspoon kosher salt

1½ cups unsweetened applesauce, such as Mott's

½ cup coarsely chopped pecans

Bourbon Cream Cheese Frosting (page 197)

Whole pecans halves, for decorating

Preheat the oven to 350 degrees. Butter a 9 × 2-inch round cake pan, line with parchment paper, then butter and flour the pan. Tap out the excess flour.

Combine the raisins and bourbon in a small bowl, cover, and microwave for 30 seconds. Set aside for 15 minutes.

Place the butter, granulated sugar, and brown sugar in the bowl of an electric mixer fitted with the paddle attachment and beat on medium speed for 3 minutes, until light and fluffy. Scrape down the bowl with a rubber spatula. With the mixer on medium, add the vanilla and the eggs, one at a time, and mix until smooth.

Meanwhile, in a medium bowl, whisk together the flour, baking soda, cinnamon, nutmeg, cloves, and salt. With the mixer on low, slowly add the flour mixture to the batter, mixing just until combined. Stir in the applesauce. Fold in the raisins (including the liquid) and chopped pecans with a rubber spatula and mix well. Pour into the prepared pan and smooth the top.

Bake for 40 to 45 minutes, until the top springs back when lightly touched and a cake tester inserted in the middle comes out clean. Cool for 30 minutes, turn out onto a cooling rack, rounded side up, and cool completely. Spread the Bourbon Cream Cheese Frosting on just the top of the cake (not the sides!) and artfully place the pecan halves on top. Serve at room temperature.

make ahead: *Bake the cake, cool it, wrap it well, and refrigerate for up to 3 days or freeze for up to 6 months. Frost the cake just before serving.*

salted pistachio meringues

This is the most astonishing way to bake meringues and it comes from Yotam Ottolenghi in London. Rather than the usual hard meringues, his have crunchy exteriors and insides like fluffy marshmallow. My addition of pistachios and salt adds great flavor and a little crunch.

MAKES 12 VERY LARGE MERINGUES

3 cups superfine or caster sugar (1 pound 5 ounces) (see note)

9 extra-large egg whites, at room temperature

1 teaspoon pure vanilla extract

⅓ cup shelled, roasted, salted pistachios, roughly chopped

Fleur de sel

Preheat the oven to 400 degrees. Arrange two racks evenly spaced in the oven.

Line a sheet pan with parchment paper and spread the sugar so it's a perfectly even thickness on the paper right to the edge of the sugar, leaving a border on the paper so the sugar doesn't spill onto the pan. Bake for 8 to 10 minutes, until the edges start to brown lightly. Watch carefully! Lower the oven to 250 degrees.

Meanwhile, place the egg whites in the bowl of an electric mixer fitted with the whisk attachment. Just before the sugar is ready, whisk the egg whites on high speed for one minute, until frothy. With the mixer on low, slowly add the hot sugar to the egg whites. (I use a large spoon at first, then pick up the paper and pour the sugar in slowly.) Add the vanilla and continue to whisk on high for 10 minutes, until the egg whites are room temperature. (The bowl may still be warm.) The meringue will be very thick and glossy.

Using two large serving spoons, scoop 6 very large, messy oval dollops of meringue onto each of two sheet pans lined with parchment paper, spacing them out because they will expand while they bake. Sprinkle the pistachios on top and bake for 1½ to 2 hours (make sure your oven isn't above 250 degrees!), until the outsides of the meringues are crisp but not browned and the centers are still soft. Sprinkle with fleur de sel and set aside to cool.

If you can't find superfine sugar, process granulated sugar in a food processor fitted with the steel blade for 5 minutes. Measure it after processing.

Don't make meringues on a rainy day or they'll come out sticky.

berries & jam milkshakes

Abby Derethik is the wonderful food stylist who works with me on my television show. One day I was walking through her kitchen and she had made jam milkshakes for the crew. These may be the most decadent drink I've ever had! Frozen berries and ice cream make this really thick and the strawberry preserves and raspberry liqueur make it intensely flavored.

SERVES 4

2 cups whole frozen strawberries (10 ounces)

1½ cups whole milk

1 cup good vanilla ice cream, such as Häagen-Dazs (see note)

7 ounces 5% plain Greek yogurt, such as Fage

6 ounces fresh raspberries, plus extra for garnish

½ cup good strawberry preserves, such as Tiptree

1 tablespoon raspberry liqueur (optional)

Soften the ice cream in the microwave for 30 seconds in order to measure it.

Place the strawberries and milk in a blender and blend on high until combined. Add the ice cream, yogurt, raspberries, strawberry preserves, and liqueur, if using, and blend on high until smooth. Pour into glasses and garnish each drink with a few raspberries. Serve ice cold.

boston cream pie

Boston Cream Pie is not a pie at all but rather a vanilla cake filled with pastry cream and topped with chocolate glaze. The cake layer is based on a cake in Cook's Illustrated *magazine that I enhanced with a hint of orange zest. Next, I made the filling with Grand Marnier and Cognac. The chocolate glaze combines bittersweet and semisweet chocolate and finally, I made four layers instead of the usual two so the proportion of cream to cake was richer. This takes a little time to make but it's so worth it!*

MAKES ONE 9-INCH CAKE /
SERVES 8

FOR THE CAKE:

¾ cup whole milk

6 tablespoons (¾ stick) unsalted butter

1½ teaspoons pure vanilla extract

½ teaspoon grated orange zest

1½ cups all-purpose flour

1½ teaspoons baking powder

1½ teaspoons kosher salt

3 extra-large eggs, at room temperature

1½ cups sugar

FOR THE SOAK:

⅓ cup freshly squeezed orange juice

⅓ cup sugar

1 tablespoon Grand Marnier

Preheat the oven to 325 degrees. Butter two 9-inch round baking pans, line them with parchment paper, butter and flour the pans, and tap out the excess flour. Set aside.

For the cake, scald the milk and butter in a small saucepan over medium heat (see note). Off the heat, add the vanilla and orange zest, cover the pan, and set aside. In a small bowl, sift together the flour, baking powder, and salt and set aside.

In the bowl of an electric mixer fitted with the paddle attachment, beat the eggs and sugar on medium-high speed for 4 minutes, until thick and light yellow and the mixture falls back on itself in a ribbon. By hand, first whisk in the warm milk mixture and then slowly whisk in the flour mixture. Don't overmix! Pour the batter evenly into the prepared pans. Bake for 22 to 25 minutes, until a toothpick comes out clean. Allow the cakes to cool in the pans for 15 minutes, then turn them out onto a baking rack, flipping them so the top sides are up. Cool to room temperature.

For the soak, combine the orange juice and sugar in a small (8-inch) sauté pan and heat until the sugar dissolves. Off the heat, add the Grand Marnier and set aside.

For the chocolate glaze, combine the heavy cream, semisweet chocolate chips, bittersweet chocolate, corn syrup, vanilla, and coffee in a heatproof bowl set over a pot of simmering water. Stir occasionally with a wooden spoon, just until the chocolates melt. Remove from the heat and set aside for 25 to 30 minutes, stirring

recipe and ingredients continue

FOR THE CHOCOLATE GLAZE:

¾ cup heavy cream

1¼ cups semisweet chocolate chips, such as Nestlé's (7½ ounces)

2 ounces bittersweet chocolate, such as Lindt, broken in pieces

2 tablespoons light corn syrup

1 teaspoon pure vanilla extract

½ teaspoon instant coffee granules, such as Nescafé

Grand Marnier Pastry Cream (recipe opposite)

To scald milk, heat it just below the boiling point—there will be small bubbles around the edge of the milk. Don't let it boil!

Don't refrigerate the assembled cake because beads of condensation will form on the chocolate.

make ahead: *Prepare the cakes and pastry cream, wrap well, and refrigerate separately. Prepare the chocolate glaze and assemble an hour before serving.*

occasionally, until the chocolate is thick enough to fall back on itself in a ribbon.

To assemble, cut both cakes in half horizontally. Place the bottom of one cake on a flat plate, cut side up. Brush it with a third of the soak. Spread a third of the Grand Marnier Pastry Cream on the cake. Place the top of the first cake on top, cut side down, and repeat with the soak and pastry cream. Place the bottom of the second cake on top, cut side up. Repeat with the soak and pastry cream. Place the top of the second cake on top, cut side down. Pour the ganache on the cake, allowing it to drip down the sides. Set aside for one hour, until the chocolate sets. Cut in wedges and serve.

grand marnier
pastry cream

5 extra-large egg yolks, at room temperature

¾ cup sugar

¼ cup cornstarch

1½ cups whole milk

1 tablespoon unsalted butter

1 tablespoon heavy cream

1 tablespoon Grand Marnier

1 teaspoon Cognac or brandy

½ teaspoon pure vanilla extract

Beat the egg yolks and sugar in the bowl of an electric mixer fitted with the paddle attachment on medium-high speed for 4 minutes, until very thick. Reduce the speed to low and add the cornstarch.

Meanwhile, scald the milk in a medium saucepan. With the mixer on low, slowly pour the hot milk into the egg mixture. Pour the mixture back into the saucepan and cook over medium-low heat for 5 to 7 minutes, stirring constantly with a wooden spoon, until the mixture starts to thicken. When the custard starts to clump on the bottom of the pan, stir constantly with a whisk (don't beat it!) to keep the custard smooth.

Cook over low heat until the custard is very thick like pudding. If you lift some custard with the whisk, it should fall back onto itself in a ribbon. Off the heat, stir in the butter, heavy cream, Grand Marnier, Cognac, and vanilla. Whisk until smooth and transfer to a bowl. Cool for 15 minutes. Place plastic wrap *directly* on the custard (not the bowl) and refrigerate until very cold.

banana rum trifle

There is a famous southern recipe called banana pudding and Magnolia Bakery in NYC makes one that everyone loves. It's layers of cream, bananas, and Nilla wafers. I decided to build on that recipe but use Ginger Snaps, dark rum, and vanilla bean to give it more flavor. No one can stop eating this!

SERVES 10

1½ cups whole milk

3 tablespoons cornstarch

¼ cup sugar

1 (14-ounce) can sweetened condensed milk

3 cups cold heavy cream

1 teaspoon pure vanilla extract

Seeds from 1 split vanilla bean

3 tablespoons dark rum, such as Mount Gay

1 (1-pound) box Nabisco Ginger Snaps, divided

6 large bananas, sliced ½ inch thick

Sweetened Whipped Cream, for decorating (page 196)

Place the milk, cornstarch, and sugar in a small saucepan and bring to a boil over medium heat, stirring constantly with a wooden spoon and scraping the bottom of the pan with the spoon. When the mixture thickens, cook for one more minute, stirring constantly. Whisk in the condensed milk and transfer to a bowl. Cover with plastic wrap and refrigerate for one hour (or up to 24 hours).

Pour the heavy cream in the bowl of an electric mixer fitted with the whisk attachment and beat on low until the cream thickens, then beat on high until it forms soft peaks. Add the milk mixture, the vanilla extract, vanilla seeds, and rum and whisk on medium for about 3 minutes, until the mixture forms soft peaks.

In a 3½-quart glass bowl with straight sides, first place one full layer of cookies (not overlapping), breaking them to fit in the spaces and making sure they touch the sides of the bowl. Add one layer of banana slices, then a quarter of the cream mixture. Continue layering cookies, bananas, and cream until you have four layers of cookies, bananas, and cream, ending with cream and swirling the top. (Save the remaining cookies for decorating.) Chill for one hour, cover with plastic wrap, and refrigerate overnight for the cookies to absorb the liquid in the cream.

Decorate with Sweetened Whipped Cream and reserved cookies and serve cold.

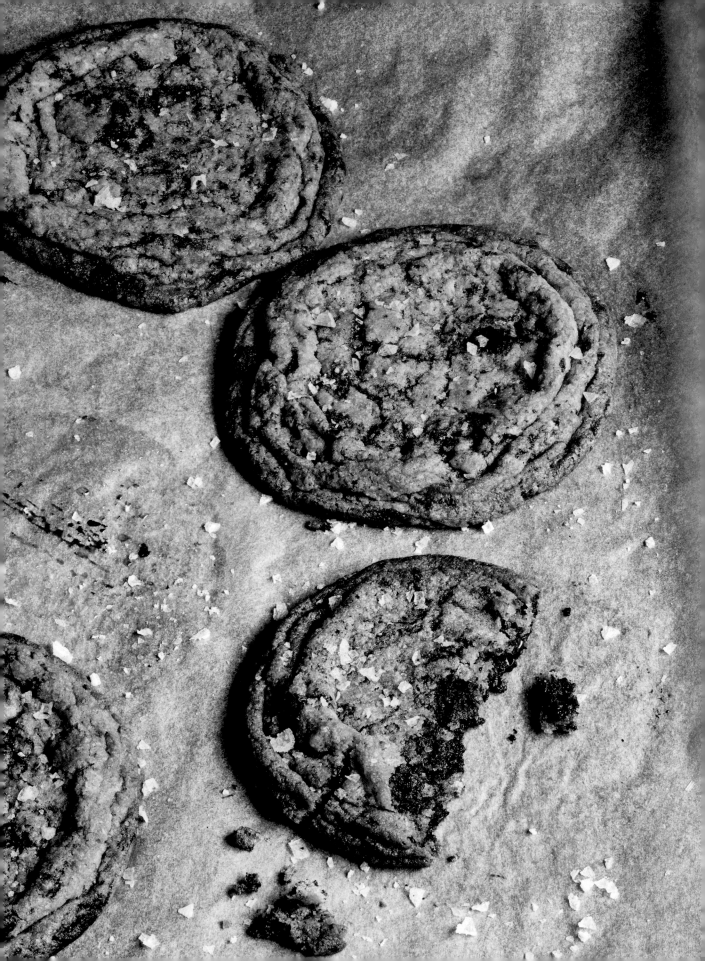

giant crinkled chocolate chip cookies

Sarah Kieffer is a food blogger who came up with the most astonishing chocolate chip cookie. Instead of handling her cookies carefully so they don't deflate, she bangs the pans on the top of the stove during baking to make rich, crispy chocolate chip cookies. These cookies are her invention but I added more chocolate and some sea salt because . . . why not??!!

MAKES 12 GIANT COOKIES

½ pound (2 sticks) unsalted butter, at room temperature

1½ cups granulated sugar

¼ cup light brown sugar, lightly packed

1 extra-large egg, at room temperature

1½ teaspoons pure vanilla extract

2 cups all-purpose flour

½ teaspoon baking soda

1 teaspoon kosher salt

8 ounces bittersweet chocolate, chopped, such as Lindt

Fleur de sel or sea salt, for sprinkling

If your oven has only two racks or you have only two sheet pans, bake these in two batches but don't freeze any batch of dough for more than 15 minutes.

Preheat the oven to 350 degrees. Arrange three racks evenly spaced in the oven (see note).

In the bowl of an electric mixer fitted with the paddle attachment, beat the butter on medium speed for 3 minutes, until creamy. Add the granulated sugar and brown sugar and beat on medium speed for 2 to 3 minutes, until light and fluffy. Scrape down the bowl with a rubber spatula. Add the egg, vanilla, and 2 tablespoons of warm water and mix on low speed just to combine. In a medium bowl, whisk together the flour, baking soda, and kosher salt. With the mixer on low, slowly add the flour mixture, then the chocolate (including the fine chocolate dust) to the batter until combined. Mix well with a rubber spatula.

With a 2¼-inch standard ice cream scoop (or ⅓ cup measure), make 12 rounded scoops of dough and place them on a sheet pan. Freeze the dough for *exactly* 15 minutes, then arrange 4 balls of dough—spaced wide apart—on each of three sheet pans lined with parchment paper. Bake for 10 minutes, until the cookies are slightly puffed in the center. Remove the pans from the oven and bang them on the stove top, until the center of the cookies deflate. Bake for 3 minutes, then bang the pans again, repeating baking and banging every 3 minutes, for 18 to 20 minutes total, until the edges of the cookies are golden brown. (The centers will be lighter and not fully cooked.) Rotate the sheet pans in the oven so the cookies bake evenly. Sprinkle the cookies with fleur de sel and cool completely on the pans.

coffee chocolate chip ice cream sandwiches

We all remember old-fashioned ice cream sandwiches; the cookie was pretty boring and the ice cream wasn't all that special, either. My assistant Lidey and I spent a fun day testing all kinds of ice cream and cookie combinations but these chocolate chip cookies with coffee chocolate chip ice cream and Heath toffee bits were everyone's favorite! Not a bad day at the office, right?

SERVES 4

1 pint coffee chocolate chip ice cream such as Talenti gelato or Häagen-Dazs Java chip

8 (2½-inch-round) crisp chocolate chip cookies, such as Tate's

½ cup Heath English Toffee Bits (see note)

Leave the gelato at room temperature for about 15 minutes, until it's soft enough to scoop but not melting. Place 4 cookies, flat sides up, on a cutting board and, using a standard (2¼-inch) ice cream scoop, put one rounded scoop of gelato on each cookie. Place the 4 remaining cookies, flat sides down, on each scoop of gelato and press lightly until the gelato spreads to the edges of the cookies.

Put the toffee bits on a small plate and, working quickly, roll the edge of each sandwich in the toffee bits, using your hand to fill in the spaces with extra toffee. Immediately, place the sandwiches in the freezer and freeze until firm. Wrap well and keep frozen until ready to serve.

You can find Heath English Toffee Bits in the baking section of the grocery store.

white chocolate toffee

Dark chocolate seems to be everyone's guilty pleasure but I prefer white chocolate, which is made from cocoa butter but with the cocoa solids removed. This is a layer of toffee topped with white chocolate, cashews, pistachios, ginger, and dried cranberries to add layers of sweet, salty, crunchy, and tart. It's a great gift to take when you're invited for dinner.

MAKES 25 TO 30 PIECES

½ pound (2 sticks) unsalted butter, plus extra for greasing the pan

1 cup sugar

1½ teaspoons pure vanilla extract

1 teaspoon kosher salt

12 ounces good white chocolate, such as Callebaut, roughly chopped

½ cup salted, roasted cashews

½ cup shelled, salted, roasted pistachios

½ cup crystallized ginger (not in syrup), ¼-inch diced (3 ounces)

½ cup dried cranberries

Fleur de sel

To melt chocolate, chop it and place it in a heatproof bowl set over a pan of simmering water, making sure the water doesn't touch the bowl. Remove from the heat before the chocolate melts completely and stir, allowing the residual heat to finish melting the chocolate.

Generously grease a 9 × 12-inch metal cake pan with butter, making sure all the sides and corners are greased. Combine the butter, sugar, vanilla, and kosher salt in a medium (10 to 11-inch) pot or Dutch oven, such as Le Creuset. Heat over medium heat, stirring occasionally, until the butter melts. Continue cooking for 8 to 10 minutes, stirring frequently with a wooden spoon, until the mixture turns a pale golden color. Continue to cook, stirring constantly, until the mixture turns a deep caramel color. (Be careful, it will be extremely hot!) Immediately pour the mixture into the prepared pan, tilting the pan to distribute it evenly. Set aside to cool for 5 minutes, then use a paring knife to score lines in large irregular serving pieces. Allow the toffee to cool for 5 minutes, then retrace the lines you drew with the paring knife.

Meanwhile, melt the white chocolate in a heatproof bowl set over a pan of simmering water (see note). Pour the chocolate over the toffee, using a spatula to spread it evenly. Immediately sprinkle on the cashews, pistachios, ginger, and cranberries so they're evenly distributed. Sprinkle with fleur de sel and set aside at room temperature for at least 2 hours, until the chocolate is completely set. Break into pieces along the scored lines and serve at room temperature.

tuscan baked apples

My friend Rolando Beramendi is an extraordinary Italian cook. I was wondering what I could do for a baked apple recipe and came across one in his book Autentico. *He bakes his apples with Vin Santo, a sweet Italian wine. I added sweetened mascarpone and caramel sauce because of course everything tastes better with mascarpone and caramel sauce.*

MAKES 6

3 tablespoons unsalted butter, plus extra to grease the pan

6 large, firm tart-sweet apples, such as Macoun or Empire

3 tablespoons turbinado sugar, such as Sugar in the Raw, divided

6 teaspoons raisins

6 teaspoons golden raisins

8 tablespoons plus 1½ cups Vin Santo wine, divided (see note)

½ cup mascarpone

1 teaspoon liquid honey

½ teaspoon pure vanilla extract

Caramel sauce, such as Fran's, warmed

Preheat the oven to 375 degrees. Butter a 9 × 12-inch ceramic baking dish just large enough to hold the apples without touching.

With a sharp paring knife, remove a 1-inch-wide ribbon of peel around the stem of each apple. With the paring knife, make five 1-inch slits around each apple, starting where the peel was removed. (This will keep the skin from exploding in the oven.) With an apple corer or 1-inch melon-baller, remove a 1¼-inch-wide column from the core three quarters of the way down the center of each apple.

Place the apples in the prepared baking dish, making sure they don't touch. In each cavity, place first 1 teaspoon of the sugar (2 tablespoons total), then 1 teaspoon raisins and 1 teaspoon golden raisins. Cut the 3 tablespoons of butter in 6 pieces and divide among the apples. Pour 1 tablespoon of the Vin Santo into each apple and 1½ cups of Vin Santo into the pan. Sprinkle the remaining 1 tablespoon of sugar on the apples.

Bake for 30 to 45 minutes, depending on the size of the apples, until they can be pierced easily with a small paring knife. Don't worry if the skins burst. (Add extra Vin Santo or water to the pan if the liquid evaporates.)

Meanwhile, in a small bowl whisk together the mascarpone, the remaining 2 tablespoons of Vin Santo, the honey, and vanilla. Cut each apple in half and serve warm with the pan juices, a drizzle of the caramel sauce, and a dollop of the mascarpone cream.

Vin Santo is a sweet Italian dessert wine. If you can't find it, use another sweet dessert wine.

chocolate-dipped brown sugar shortbread

I adore any form of shortbread, which is a classic, simple butter cookie. This updated version is baked in fingers, dipped in milk chocolate, and sprinkled with pecans. They remind everyone of Pepperidge Farm Milano cookies, but they're so much better!

MAKES 30 TO 36 COOKIES

¾ pound (3 sticks) unsalted butter, at room temperature

1 cup light brown sugar, lightly packed

2 teaspoons pure vanilla extract

3 cups all-purpose flour

1 teaspoon kosher salt

FOR THE CHOCOLATE COATING:

1 cup milk chocolate morsels, such as Hershey's (6 ounces)

6 tablespoons (¾ stick) unsalted butter

½ cup toasted pecans, minced and lightly salted

Preheat the oven to 350 degrees. Arrange two racks evenly spaced in the oven.

Place the butter and brown sugar in the bowl of an electric mixer fitted with a paddle attachment and mix on medium speed *just* until the butter and sugar are combined so you don't whip a lot of air into it. With the mixer on low, add the vanilla and scrape down the bowl with a rubber spatula. In a separate bowl, sift together the flour and salt. With the mixer on low, slowly add the flour mixture to the butter and sugar mixture and mix just until the dough comes together.

Scoop out 1-ounce pieces of dough (about a tablespoon), roll each one into a ball, then roll it into a 2½-inch-long log. Place the logs 2 inches apart on two sheet pans lined with parchment paper and bake for 15 to 17 minutes, until the cookies start to brown around the edges and spring back when lightly touched. Set aside to cool on the pans.

For the coating, place the chocolate and the butter in a heatproof bowl and microwave on high for 30 seconds. Stir the mixture vigorously and continue to microwave in 30-second increments until the chocolate is just melted.

Drag half of the rounded top of each cookie through the chocolate and place it, chocolate side up, on a piece of parchment paper. While the chocolate is still warm, sprinkle on the pecans. Repeat with all the cookies. Set aside for at least 30 minutes for the chocolate to firm.

breakfast

smashed eggs on toast

—

whole-grain breakfast bowl

—

breakfast tacos

—

buckwheat crêpes "complète"

—

creamed spinach & eggs

—

apple cinnamon dutch baby

—

bacon, egg & cheddar sandwich

—

fresh raspberry mini corn muffins

—

waffle iron hash browns

—

chunky apple butter

—

vanilla cold-brewed iced coffee

—

wake up for breakfast

I don't know about you but I tend to eat the same thing for breakfast every morning for about ten years, until I can't eat it one more day—and then I switch to something *else* for the next ten years. It needs to be easy enough to prepare while I'm half asleep, fairly healthy (why start the day off on the wrong foot?), and of course it needs to be delicious or I won't get out of bed. Right now, I've been on an Irish oatmeal kick with a splash of milk and a drizzle of maple syrup. It's hot, it's satisfying, and I can make it in 4 minutes in the microwave. But I'm thinking it might be time for something new.

For each recipe in this section, I went back to the classic comfort breakfast foods that we all love, from scrambled eggs and poached eggs to waffles, oatmeal, and pancakes but thought about a new, more modern way to prepare each one. Some are just tweaks on an old favorite, such as Vanilla Cold-Brewed Iced Coffee (page 246), which you make overnight in the fridge but the coffee flavor is so much more interesting and less acidic than classic iced coffee. Others are big changes, though. Instead of making waffles, I used my waffle iron to make Waffle Iron Hash Browns (page 242) that are the tenderest and crispiest I've ever made. We've all had poached eggs on toast but for my Smashed Eggs on Toast (page 226), I toasted the bread and made perfect 6½-minute jammy eggs that I roughly chopped up and served on the toast with fresh dill and coarse mustard. It's easier than poaching eggs and so much more delicious! I also wanted to have a breakfast sandwich and discovered a way to cook the eggs in a microwave, then put them on toasted English muffins with bacon, cheese, and avocado—a perfect breakfast sandwich in no time at all. (It's also not a bad "breakfast for dinner" option!)

When I ran my specialty food store, Barefoot Contessa, we used to make a lot of muffins. On Saturdays in the summer, we would bake a thousand muffins a day and we'd still run out! The bakers would come out of the kitchen carrying trays of freshly baked muffins and before they were three steps through the door, customers would start grabbing muffins right off their trays. From that experience, I learned that you could make muffin batter the night before and then just scoop and bake the muffins in the morning. It's a great trick to do at home so you don't have to worry about measuring and mixing the batter while you're still half asleep. My Fresh Raspberry Mini Corn Muffins (page 241) are made, of course, with lots of fresh raspberries and stone-ground cornmeal that give the muffins so much texture and flavor, plus milk and butter to keep them moist all day long.

I hope you find lots of new satisfying breakfasts that you'll want to eat every day of the week and some that you'll even want to get up a little early to make for your guests.

smashed eggs on toast

Is there anything simpler or more satisfying than poached eggs on toast? This variation is simply soft-boiled eggs chopped on toast with lots of fresh dill and whole-grain mustard. There are all kinds of ways to make soft-boiled "jammy" eggs but this is the easiest: 6½ minutes in a pot of boiling water and you're done!

SERVES 4

8 cold extra-large eggs

8 (½-inch-thick) slices from a white bread or Pullman loaf

4 tablespoons (½ stick) unsalted butter, at room temperature

4 teaspoons whole-grain mustard

4 teaspoons minced fresh dill

Kosher salt and freshly ground black pepper

Coarse sea salt or fleur de sel

To toast bread in the oven, place the slices in one layer on two sheet pans and bake at 400 degrees for 12 to 15 minutes, turning once, until golden brown.

Fill a large saucepan with water and bring it to a full rolling boil over medium-high heat. With a slotted spoon, carefully lower the eggs, one at a time, into the water. (Don't allow them to fall into the pot or the shells will crack!) Lower the heat and cook for exactly 6½ minutes (not 6 minutes and not 7 minutes), adjusting the temperature to maintain a low simmer. (If the water is boiling, the eggs will knock against each other and crack.) Carefully transfer the eggs to a bowl of ice water for *exactly* 2 minutes. Remove the eggs from the water and peel (page 91).

Meanwhile, toast the bread in a toaster or oven (see note) and place the slices on a cutting board. Spread each slice first with ½ tablespoon of the butter and then ½ teaspoon of the mustard.

Place one egg on each slice of toast and chop the eggs roughly without cutting into the bread (the bread will absorb the runny yolks). Sprinkle with dill, kosher salt, and pepper. Sprinkle with coarse sea salt and serve warm.

whole-grain breakfast bowl

I usually have a bowl of oatmeal for breakfast but once in a while, I feel like something more interesting. This is oatmeal but with a whole lot more texture and flavor. The chewy barley is a good contrast to the creamy oatmeal, and sweet dates, fresh raspberries, and crunchy hazelnuts are so satisfying first thing in the morning!

SERVES 4

1 cup pearled barley (see note)

1½ teaspoons kosher salt

½ cup old-fashioned rolled oats, such as Bob's Red Mill

½ cup whole milk, plus extra for serving

½ cup medium-diced pitted, dried dates (6 to 8 dates)

6 ounces fresh raspberries

⅓ cup chopped toasted hazelnuts (see note)

Pure maple syrup, for serving

Make sure you buy "pearled" barley, which has been processed so it cooks faster.

To toast hazelnuts, place them in a small (8-inch) dry sauté pan over medium heat and cook for 3 to 5 minutes, tossing often, until fragrant. Cool slightly, rub the nuts on a board to remove some of the skins, and chop.

Combine the barley, salt, and 2 cups water in a medium saucepan. Bring to a boil, lower the heat, and simmer covered for 30 minutes. Add the oats plus 2 cups water, return to a boil, lower the heat, and simmer covered for 20 minutes, until the barley is tender and the oats are creamy. Off the heat, stir in ½ cup milk.

Spoon the barley and oats into four shallow bowls. Sprinkle with the dates, raspberries, and hazelnuts, drizzle with maple syrup, and pour on some milk. Serve hot.

breakfast tacos

Kristina Felix Ibarra works with me and she's a great cook. We were thinking about breakfast recipes and she suggested her favorite breakfast tacos. Corn tortillas, scrambled eggs, Monterey Jack cheese, and avocado—who wouldn't want that for breakfast??

SERVES 4

1½ tablespoons unsalted butter

6 scallions, thinly sliced, white and green parts separated

8 extra-large eggs

Kosher salt and freshly ground black pepper

8 (6-inch) white corn tortillas

8 ounces Monterey Jack cheese, grated

1 ripe Hass avocado, pitted, peeled, and thinly sliced

Chipotle hot sauce or Tabasco

Melt the butter in a small (9-inch) sauté pan over medium heat. Add the white parts of the scallions (reserving the greens) and sauté for 3 to 4 minutes, until almost tender.

Meanwhile, whisk together the eggs and 2 teaspoons salt in a medium bowl and add them to the pan. Cook over medium-low heat for 5 minutes, stirring almost constantly. When the eggs are almost set, turn off the heat and allow the residual heat in the pan to finish the cooking.

Meanwhile, heat a cast-iron skillet over medium heat. When it's very hot, add a tortilla and toast for one minute. Turn the tortilla over and sprinkle 1 ounce of the cheese on top. After the cheese melts, transfer the taco to a plate. Repeat for all 8 tacos, placing two tacos on each plate.

To serve, spoon an eighth of the scrambled eggs down the middle of each taco. Add slices of avocado and the reserved scallion greens. Sprinkle with hot sauce, salt, and pepper and serve warm.

buckwheat crêpes "complète"

One of my favorite restaurants in New York City is La Mercerie run by French chef Marie-Aude Rose. Her food is French—both country and elegant. This is my version of her amazing buckwheat crêpes with Black Forest ham, nutty Gruyère, and a fried egg. It's great for breakfast, lunch, or brunch.

MAKES 6 CRÊPES

1 cup whole milk

1 tablespoon unsalted butter, melted

8 extra-large eggs, divided

¾ cup whole-grain buckwheat flour, such as Bob's Red Mill

¼ cup all-purpose flour

Kosher salt and freshly ground black pepper

4 tablespoons (½ stick) unsalted butter, divided

6 large, thin slices Black Forest ham

3 cups grated Gruyère cheese (8 to 10 ounces)

½ cup crème fraîche whisked with 1 tablespoon milk

Minced fresh parsley

To keep the yolks intact, I break each egg into a small bowl and slide it into the pan without touching the other eggs.

Put the milk, melted butter, 2 of the eggs, the buckwheat flour, all-purpose flour, and 1½ teaspoons salt in the jar of a blender and process for 30 seconds, until smooth. Refrigerate in the covered jar for at least 3 hours or up to 24 hours. Before making the crêpes, add ⅓-cup water and blend until smooth.

Preheat the oven to 350 degrees. Arrange three racks evenly spaced in the oven.

Heat a 9-inch nonstick crêpe pan over medium heat, add 1 teaspoon of the butter, and swirl it with a paper towel. Pour a full ⅓-cup measuring cup of batter into the pan and swirl it to distribute the batter evenly. Cook the crêpe on one side only for 1½ to 2 minutes, until it's cooked through and doesn't stick to the pan. (Don't flip it over.) Transfer the crêpe to a sheet pan lined with parchment paper. Make 5 more crêpes with the remaining batter, adding butter to keep the crêpes from sticking to the pan and placing 2 crêpes on each of the three sheet pans lined with parchment paper. Place one slice of ham on each crêpe and sprinkle each with ½ cup of the Gruyère.

To fry the eggs, heat a medium (10 to 11-inch) sauté pan over medium-low heat and add 1 tablespoon of the butter. When the butter is sizzling, carefully add 3 of the eggs without breaking the yolks (see note) and fry them for 4 to 6 minutes, until the whites are almost done but the yolks are still runny. Place one egg, sunny side up, at 12 o'clock on each crêpe and repeat with 1 tablespoon of the butter and the remaining 3 eggs. Sprinkle the eggs generously with salt and pepper and bake the crêpes for 5 minutes, until the cheese melts. While the cheese is hot, fold the sides of each crêpe toward the middle, overlapping like a letter, pressing lightly, with the egg yolk visible. Drizzle each crêpe with the crème fraîche mixture, sprinkle with parsley and salt, and serve hot.

creamed spinach & eggs

I've always loved Wolfgang Puck's restaurants Cut because he does a modern take on a traditional American steakhouse, serving side dishes such as tempura onion rings and truffled French fries to go with the amazing steaks. This creamed spinach with fried eggs on top is inspired by one of Wolfgang's sides but I thought it would also make a great breakfast or brunch. I serve this with crusty bread or toast.

SERVES 4

2 tablespoons unsalted butter

2 tablespoons good olive oil

½ cup minced shallots (2 shallots)

1¼ pounds fresh baby spinach, washed and spun dry

1 (5.2-ounce) package Boursin Garlic and Fine Herbs cheese

⅓ cup heavy cream

Pinch of ground nutmeg

Kosher salt and freshly ground black pepper

4 extra-large eggs

⅓ cup grated Gruyère cheese (1 ounce)

1 tablespoon freshly grated Italian Parmesan cheese

Crack each egg into a small bowl and slide it onto the spinach to avoid breaking the yolk.

Preheat the oven to 400 degrees.

Heat the butter and olive oil in a large (12-inch) sauté pan over medium heat. Add the shallots and cook for 3 to 5 minutes, until tender. Add the spinach in large handfuls, tossing with metal tongs to wilt each batch before adding another. After all of the spinach has been added and completely wilted, crumble the Boursin into the spinach and add the cream, nutmeg, 1 teaspoon salt, and ½ teaspoon pepper. Cook for 3 minutes, stirring often, until the cheese and cream form a sauce.

Transfer the spinach mixture to a 9 × 9-inch square or 8 × 10-inch oval baking dish. With the back of a wooden spoon, make four indentations in the spinach. Place an egg in each indentation (see note). Sprinkle the eggs with salt and pepper. Sprinkle the spinach and eggs with the Gruyère and Parmesan. Bake for 12 to 13 minutes for runny yolks or 13 to 14 minutes for yolks that are just cooked. Serve hot from the baking dish.

apple cinnamon dutch baby

A Dutch baby is a kind of pancake. I like them because they're delicious and so dramatic to serve—this one is made with apples and cinnamon and it gets puffed and browned on the edges. In order for the pancake to puff up properly, the pan needs to be very hot when you pour in the batter.

SERVES 2 TO 4

1 large Granny Smith apple

4 tablespoons (½ stick) unsalted butter, divided

2 tablespoons granulated sugar, divided

¼ teaspoon ground cinnamon

½ cup whole milk

2 extra-large eggs, at room temperature

½ teaspoon pure vanilla extract

½ cup all-purpose flour

¼ teaspoon kosher salt

Confectioners' sugar

Pure maple syrup, for serving

The oven temperature is important for a Dutch baby so test your oven with a thermometer.

Preheat the oven to 425 degrees (see note).

Peel, core, and slice the apple ⅛ inch thick. Melt 3 tablespoons of the butter in a 9-inch ovenproof crêpe pan or skillet over medium to medium-high heat. Add the apple, 1 tablespoon of the granulated sugar, and the cinnamon and toss well. Sauté the apple for 5 to 7 minutes until tender, tossing occasionally. Spread the apple out in the pan and keep hot over low heat.

Meanwhile, melt the remaining tablespoon of butter in the microwave. In a medium bowl, whisk together the milk, eggs, melted butter, and vanilla. In a small bowl, combine the flour, the remaining tablespoon of granulated sugar, and the salt. Whisk the flour mixture into the milk mixture, whisking until there are no lumps. Pour the batter over the cooked apple in the hot pan and immediately place in the oven.

Bake for 12 to 15 minutes, until the pancake is puffed and the edges start to get crispy and browned. Dust lightly with sifted confectioners' sugar, cut in wedges, and serve hot with maple syrup.

bacon, egg & cheddar sandwich

I wanted to make a breakfast sandwich that would be amazing but easy enough to prepare in the morning. The trick is combining the eggs with good sharp Cheddar and cooking them in the microwave! Then it all goes on a big English muffin with bacon and avocado. Done!

SERVES 2

2 slices thick-cut applewood-smoked bacon, such as Nodine's

Good olive oil

4 extra-large eggs

2 tablespoons whole milk

Kosher salt and freshly ground black pepper

4 tablespoons grated sharp white Cheddar, divided

2 fork-split sandwich-size English muffins

½ ripe Hass avocado, pitted, peeled, and thinly sliced

To cook the bacon, heat a large (12-inch) sauté pan over medium heat. Add the bacon and cook for 5 to 7 minutes, turning occasionally, until nicely browned. Transfer to a plate lined with paper towels and set aside.

Meanwhile, generously brush two small microwavable bowls (about 4 inches in diameter) with olive oil and set aside. In a *separate* bowl, beat together the eggs, milk, ½ teaspoon salt, and ¼ teaspoon pepper. Pour half of the egg mixture into each of the two oiled bowls and microwave on high for 30 seconds. Stir the eggs gently with a fork to combine the cooked parts with the uncooked parts. Continue to microwave and stir at 30-second intervals, until the eggs are puffed and almost cooked through. Sprinkle 1 tablespoon of the Cheddar in each bowl and microwave for 30 seconds to melt the cheese and finish cooking the eggs.

Meanwhile, toast the English muffins until nicely browned. Place the bottom half of each toasted English muffin on a plate. Layer half of the avocado slices on each one and sprinkle with salt and pepper. Break the bacon strips in half and place two halves on each sandwich. Slide the eggs, cheese side up, on top of the bacon, and sprinkle a tablespoon of the remaining Cheddar on each sandwich. Sprinkle with salt and pepper and cover with the tops of the toasted English muffins. Serve hot.

fresh raspberry mini corn muffins

I can't write a cookbook about comfort food without including corn muffins; they're my guilty pleasure. Corn muffins can be dry and tasteless but allowing the batter to sit for 15 minutes gives the dry ingredients time to absorb the wet ones and results in moister muffins. This is a variation on my favorite Raspberry Corn Muffins from The Barefoot Contessa Cookbook *made with fresh raspberries instead of raspberry jam.*

48 MINI MUFFINS

Baking spray with flour, such as Pam

3 cups all-purpose flour

1 cup granulated sugar

1 cup fine cornmeal, such as Indian Head

2 tablespoons baking powder

1 tablespoon kosher salt

2 cups whole milk

2 extra-large eggs

½ pound (2 sticks) unsalted butter, melted

12 ounces firm fresh raspberries

2 tablespoons turbinado sugar, such as Sugar in the Raw

make ahead: *Prepare the batter completely, cover, and refrigerate. Scoop and bake the next day.*

Preheat the oven to 375 degrees. Arrange two racks evenly spaced in the oven. Generously spray two mini muffin pans (24 mini muffins each) with the baking spray, including the tops of the pans.

In a large bowl, whisk together the flour, granulated sugar, cornmeal, baking powder, and salt. In a separate bowl whisk together the milk, eggs, and butter. Make a well in the middle of the dry ingredients, pour the wet ingredients into the well, and stir with a rubber spatula, *just* until combined. (Don't worry if it's a little lumpy.) Set the batter aside for 15 minutes.

When the batter has rested, fold the raspberries into the batter with the spatula. With a small (1¾-inch) ice cream scoop (you can also use a spoon), fill each muffin cup with a rounded scoop of batter, making sure each one contains some raspberries. Sprinkle the full 2 tablespoons of turbinado sugar on the muffins.

Bake for 20 minutes, until the muffins spring back when gently touched and a cake tester comes out clean. Serve warm or at room temperature.

waffle iron hash browns

*Cooking anything other than waffles in a waffle iron isn't something I would normally
do but these hash browns come out so tender and crispy! A Belgian waffle iron makes big
tender hash browns and a regular waffle iron makes them a little thinner and crisper.
Both are fantastic!*

**MAKES 8 HASH BROWNS /
SERVES 4 TO 6**

1½ pounds russet (baking)
potatoes, peeled (2 large)

1 medium yellow onion

2 tablespoons melted butter,
plus extra for the waffle iron

1 extra-large egg, lightly beaten

1 tablespoon all-purpose flour

Kosher salt and freshly ground
black pepper

Preheat the oven to 250 degrees. Preheat a Belgian or
standard waffle iron on medium-high heat.

Grate the potatoes in a food processor fitted with the
grating disk. (You can also grate them by hand on a box
grater as you would grate carrots.) Transfer the potatoes
to a clean kitchen towel and spread them out. Working
quickly, roll the towel up like a jelly roll. Press firmly
to squeeze out any moisture but not so hard that you
break up the potatoes. Transfer the potatoes to a large
mixing bowl. Grate the onion the same way you grated
the potatoes, spreading it out on the kitchen towel
and squeezing out the moisture. Add the onion to the
bowl. Add the butter, egg, flour, 1½ teaspoons salt, and
½ teaspoon pepper and mix with a fork.

When the waffle iron is hot, brush both sides generously
with melted butter. Place a generous ⅓ cup of the potato
mixture on each of the four waffle divisions, spreading
it out with a fork. Cook for 5 to 10 minutes, depending
on your waffle iron, until the potatoes are browned
and crispy. Transfer the potatoes, browner side up, to a
sheet pan lined with parchment paper and keep warm
in the oven for up to 30 minutes while you prepare the
next batch. Repeat with the remaining mixture to make
8 hash browns. Transfer to a platter, sprinkle with salt,
and serve hot.

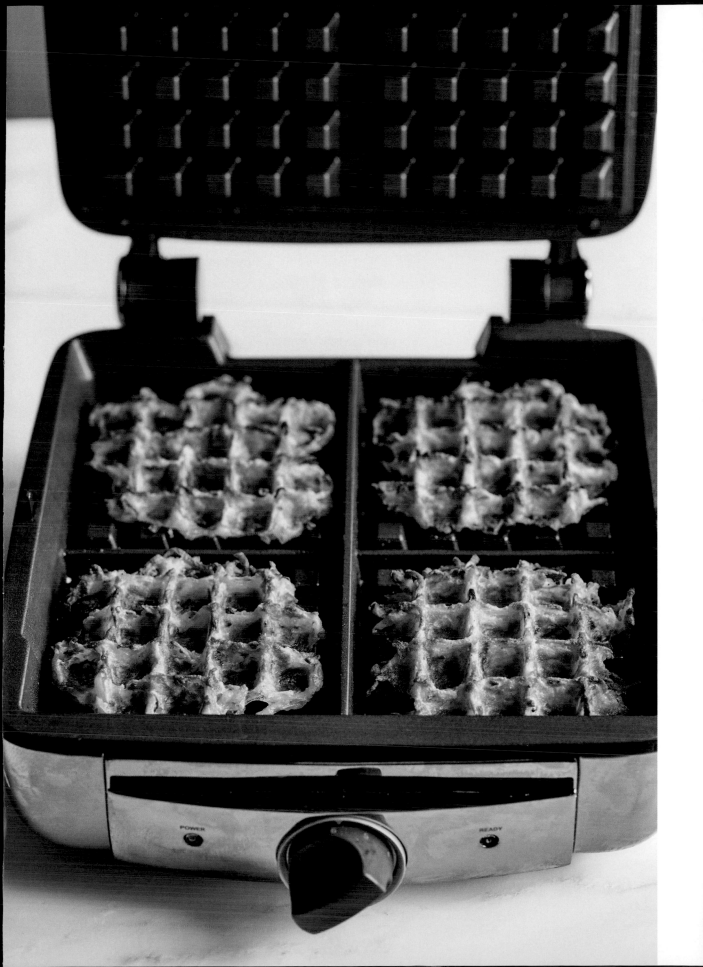

chunky apple butter

A pleasing texture is a big part of what makes something delicious. Most commercial apple butters are just puréed apples with spices. My fresh apple butter is chunky and made with both sweet and tart apples that are cooked slowly in butter to caramelize the sugars. Then I add lots of brown sugar, apple cider, and autumn spices. When apples are available at farm stands, this is a treat to serve on whole-grain toast for breakfast.

MAKES 3 CUPS

6 tablespoons (¾ stick) unsalted butter

1 cup light brown sugar, lightly packed

1½ pounds Granny Smith apples (3 large)

1 pound crisp sweet red apples, such as Macoun or Empire (2 large)

1½ cups fresh apple cider

1½ teaspoons ground cinnamon

¼ teaspoon ground cloves

¼ teaspoon ground allspice

½ vanilla bean, split lengthwise

In a medium (9 to 10-inch) pot or Dutch oven, such as Le Creuset, melt the butter and sugar together and cook over low heat for 5 minutes. Meanwhile, peel, core, and dice all the apples in 1-inch chunks. Add the apples to the pot along with the apple cider, cinnamon, cloves, allspice, and vanilla bean. Bring to a boil, lower the heat, cover, and simmer for 15 minutes, until the apples are very tender. Uncover the pot and simmer for 35 to 40 minutes longer, until the apples are completely soft and the liquid is reduced.

Discard the vanilla bean and transfer the apples, including any liquid, to the bowl of a food processor fitted with the steel blade. Pulse the processor just 5 times, until the mixture is a chunky purée. Transfer to a container and refrigerate for up to 2 weeks.

For serving, heat in a microwave for one minute and serve at room temperature or slightly warmed so the butter in the apple butter is not congealed.

vanilla cold-brewed iced coffee

I love cold-brewed coffee because it's less acidic than regular coffee. However, without the right equipment, it can be seriously messy and cumbersome. You can certainly do this with a large coffee cone and filter, but my assistant Kristina introduced me to the CoffeeSock, which is a glass jar with a cloth bag to hold the coffee grinds, and I was totally hooked! Iced coffee with a hint of vanilla is the perfect afternoon pick-me-up.

SERVES 6 TO 8

2 cups coarsely ground Colombian coffee (5 ounces) (see note)

1 teaspoon pure vanilla extract

Ice, whole milk, and sugar, for serving

A 64-ounce CoffeeSock DIY ColdBrew Kit is available on Amazon.com.

I use medium-roasted regular or decaf Colombian coffee beans ground on the coarsest setting of a commercial coffee grinder.

If you're using a coffee cone and coffee filter, combine the coffee and 64 ounces of cold tap water, cover, and refrigerate overnight. The next day, pour the mixture through a large coffee cone lined with a large coffee filter into a jar or pitcher, until all the coffee has drained through. Discard the grounds. Add the vanilla to the coffee. Fill tall glasses halfway with ice and pour on the cold coffee. Stir in milk and sugar, to taste, and serve ice cold.

If you're using the CoffeeSock, place the CoffeeSock in the jar and fold the top over the neck of the jar. Spoon the coffee into the sock, add 1 cup cold tap water to wet the grounds completely, and allow it to sit for 60 seconds. Tie the sock as directed and put the sock into the jar. Fill the jar with cold tap water, close and secure the lid, and refrigerate for 12 hours.

Remove the CoffeeSock and squeeze it to leave as much of the cold-brewed coffee in the jar as possible. Discard the coffee grounds and stir in the vanilla. Fill tall glasses halfway with ice and pour on the cold coffee. Stir in milk and sugar, to taste, and serve ice cold.

sources

sources

Roman & Williams Guild
53 Howard Street
New York, New York
10013
212-852-9099

Bloom
43 Madison Street
Sag Harbor, New York
11963
631-725-5940

French Presse
160 Main Street
Amagansett, New York
11930
631-604-1455

Ted Muehling
52 White Street
New York, New York
10013
212-431-3825

Hudson Grace
3350 Sacramento Street
San Francisco, California
94118
415-440-7400

David Mellor available at Didriks and Local Root
Belmont Center
77 Leonard Street
Belmont, Massachusetts
02478
617-354-5700

Caravane Saint Paul
6 rue Pavée
Paris, France 75004
011 33 1 44 61 04 20
For other locations, see caravane.fr.

CB2
979 Third Avenue
New York, New York
10022
212-355-7974
For locations nationwide, see cb2.com/stores.

index

Note: Page references in *italics* indicate photographs.

recipe index